FLIGHT ATTENDANT

FLIGHT ATTENDANT

Future Aviation Professionals of America
with
David Massey

New York London Toronto
Sydney Tokyo Singapore

Copyright © 1990 by Future Aviation Professionals of America
All rights reserved
including the right of reproduction
in whole or in part in any form

 ARCO

Simon & Schuster, Inc.
15 Columbus Circle
New York, NY 10023

DISTRIBUTED BY PRENTICE HALL TRADE SALES

Designed by Future Aviation Professionals of America
Manufactured in the United States of America

1 2 3 4 5 6 7 8 9 10

Library of Congress Cataloging-in-Publication Data

Flight attendant / Future Aviation Professionals of America with David
   Massey
        p. cm
   ISBN 0-13-322942-4
   1. Flight attendants—Vocational guidance.   I. Massey, David,
1940-   . II. Future Aviation Professionals of America.
HD8039.A43F55 1990
387.7'42—dc20   90-32484
                                                                      CIP

Contents

Introduction vii

PART ONE — THE FLIGHT ATTENDANT PROFESSION

    Chapter 1 - That Reassuring Presence **3**
    Chapter 2 - The Flight Attendant's World **7**
    Chapter 3 - Should You Become a Flight Attendant? **19**
    Chapter 4 - The Job Market Today **29**

PART TWO — YOUR JOB SEARCH

    Chapter 5 - Getting Started: Resumes and Letters **51**
    Chapter 6 - The Application Process **67**
    Chapter 7 - Fine-Tuning Your Image **75**
    Chapter 8 - Preparing Yourself Mentally **99**
    Chapter 9 - Types of Interviews **105**
    Chapter 10 - The Day of Your Interview **137**
    Chapter 11 - Really Following Up **149**

PART THREE — BEGINNING YOUR CAREER

    Chapter 12 - Your Training **159**
    Chapter 13 - The Workplace **169**
    Chapter 14 - Probation, Domicile, Reserve Status **181**
    Chapter 15 - Onward and Upward **189**

APPENDIX A – FAA REGULATIONS
AFFECTING FLIGHT ATTENDANTS **193**

APPENDIX B – FLIGHT ATTENDANT
DIRECTORY OF EMPLOYERS **209**

GLOSSARY **221**

INTRODUCTION

The primary purpose of this book is to assist you in maximizing your potential for employment as a professional flight attendant and to provide information that will help you reach your career-goal job.

We will assume that your career goal is to find employment as a professional flight attendant with a major, national, turbojet or regional airline. The following chapters discuss matters that will affect your competitiveness, as well as how to conduct a job search. They deal with the airline jobs themselves and answer some frequently asked questions about pursuing an aviation career. Since most of the better jobs are with the airlines, the bulk of discussion deals with the airline industry. The authors believe this information, plus the data on the various charts, will make you more knowledgeable and successful as you pursue your goal.

Part I

THE FLIGHT ATTENDANT PROFESSION

CHAPTER 1

That Reassuring Presence

There is a reassuring presence in the sky that has become such a part of flying that it is almost taken for granted. In the booming occupation of commercial flying, the career of flight attendant is booming right along with it.

Today's flight attendant is a highly trained professional in one of the most dynamic industries in the world. She — or, in many cases, he — has the advantages of excellent pay, a lot of time off, liberal job benefits, and the adventure of a life that does not get mired down in a rut.

By mid-1989, the average length of service of flight attendants had risen to seven years, from only two a decade earlier. Flight attendants today view their positions as careers, not just jobs. Most of them are dedicated to their work and, by an overwhelming 74 percent in one survey, are committed to remaining with their present airline employers until retirement.

The job today is a far cry from its rather quaint beginnings in 1930, when a scarcity of passengers for the infant airline industry created a need for the first "stewardesses," as flight attendants were called then. Ellen Church, the very first flight attendant, served chicken dinners to the meager clientele on a 12-passenger piston-engine plane flown by her employer, Boeing Air Transport (a predecessor of United Airlines). The idea of having Ms. Church aboard was that if Boeing included in the crew of the airplane a young woman — specifically, a trained, registered nurse — the public would be encouraged to fly.

Today, the position of flight attendant is shaped by strong demand for airline travel, rather than by the absence of demand that created the position. In keeping with the high customer contact of the position in a booming service industry, flight attendants must acquire a variety of technical, psychological and social skills in addition to a knowledge of first aid and emergency procedures.

Yet, except for the greater sophistication of the knowledge and skills required, the essential role of the flight attendant is the same: to aid passenger safety and comfort and to provide a reassuring presence that helps to give passengers the feelings of security and pleasure which are necessary for wide public acceptance of air travel.

Flight attendants obviously have been doing their job well. They have helped make people feel at ease with flying, and the latter part of the 20th Century has brought greater popularity of air travel than ever before.

A Peek at One Flight

Oddly enough, as much as people love to fly, they know very little about what goes into the making of a flight. "A passenger recently asked me what the flight crew must do in preparing for and conducting a flight," a manager at a small airline said. "As I began to answer the question, I realized the preparations could take longer than actually flying the trip.

"The trip begins with check-in," the manager said. "The captain, first officer and flight attendant meet and discuss the plan for the day. The captain then will call flight operations and talk with the dispatcher. Their discussion includes weather, fuel loads, passenger loads, alternate airports, and aircraft swaps. Once they agree on these matters, the dispatcher will issue a flight release authorizing the captain to conduct the flight as planned. The captain will then sign the release, obtain hard copies of actual and forecast weather, and proceed to the aircraft.

"By this time, the first officer and flight attendant are already out at the aircraft conducting exterior and cabin pre-flight inspections and supervising the refueling and catering. Ten minutes prior to departure, the passengers are boarded, last-minute baggage is loaded, and the cockpit crew begins preparing for engine start. Prior to engine start, the first officer will call clearance delivery and request a clearance to the destination. This call confirms the route of flight and the altitude to be flown.

"Once that is completed, the first of 11 checklists required during the flight will be performed. Weight and balance, takeoff speeds and power settings are now determined and written on a reference card that the crew will use during the flight. On a small airline, the flight attendant often has to understand weight and balance and superintend much of the pre-flight activity in this regard.

"After engine start, the first officer will call ramp and ground control for taxi clearance. As the crew members are taxiing for takeoff, they will perform the pre-takeoff checklist, followed by the takeoff checklist. The flight attendant at this time is making the required passenger briefing and preparing the cabin for takeoff.

"Once the plane is airborne, there are more checklists, communications with air traffic control, and constant monitoring of aircraft systems and flight progress. The actual time the aircraft leaves the gate, as well as actual takeoff time, is recorded on a flight log and reported via radio to ground personnel, who enter the information into the computer system of the small carrier's major airline partner. Another radio call is made to the destination station 10 minutes prior to landing. Any request for fuel, catering, or passenger assistance is made at this time.

"When the plane has landed and passengers have deplaned, the process starts all over again.

"For the flight attendant as well as the pilots, however, the trips actually begin even before check-in. Rules about being on time for flights are rigid, and a missed flight can be cause for dismissal."

The account from the airline manager was necessarily sketchy, especially in regard to the flight attendant's role. No description of flight attendant duties on a given flight could be complete without a reportorial blow-by-blow account. While every flight attendant has the same basic duties, responsibilities of the position vary, depending upon the size of the airline and its company policies with regard to cabin and in-flight procedures.

The following remarks are general ones, couched to cover a variety of working environments at carriers ranging from small to major airlines. Therefore, they represent a "shotgun" attempt to describe situations as different as the single-attendant flight on an 18-passenger British Aerospace Jetstream 31 to a 16-attendant transoceanic flight on a Boeing 747.

A flight attendant's primary responsibility is the control and maintenance of passengers' safety at all times. Before the passengers are boarded, she or he has the responsibility of checking the emergency equipment aboard the airplane to make sure it is in good working condition. Equipment to be checked includes evacuation slides, oxygen bottles, life vests, fire extinguishers, and other emergency equipment. Once the passengers are seated, the cabin must be inspected to ensure that seat belts are fastened, that seat belts in unoccupied seats are correctly positioned, and that carry-on luggage is properly stowed. The galley and serving equipment also must be prepared for takeoff.

All flight attendants are trained in first aid and emergency procedures associated with the aircraft in which they will be working. They are instructed in the federal safety regulations that govern all air carriers. In an emergency, they are counted on for their knowledge, leadership and quick thinking. There are even circumstances under which the flight attendants, rather than the captain, will initiate an evacuation. One airline's in-flight manual states that in "a situation where the flight attendants must take immediate action in the interest of safety, the attendants will attempt to contact the cockpit prior to initiating an evacuation. If conditions exist where danger is obvious and imminent and contact with the cockpit is not possible, the flight attendants will signal the cockpit with four (4) chimes and initiate the evacuation."

In-flight service begins when the flight attendant or attendants board the aircraft. There may or may not already be passengers on board (continuing passengers from a previous flight). Each flight attendant has his or her own duties to accomplish prior to the boarding of local passengers. Depending on the size of the aircraft, one to 16 flight attendants will come aboard. At this point, those flight attendants responsible for the galley will be receiving fresh supplies from the local commissary; they must ensure that they have what they need for the services planned on this flight.

Passengers are greeted at the door as they board and are helped to settle safely and comfortably for the flight. If there are first-class passengers, they may be offered something to drink before takeoff. Sometimes there is time to offer magazines to the passengers before takeoff.

Weight and balance computation is based on customer seating assignments. One flight attendant will have the responsibility of ensuring that an accurate customer count is delivered to the captain as soon as possible prior to pushback (on a jet) or taxi toward the runway (on a turboprop). On large aircraft, the count must differentiate between first/business class count and coach count. If a "half-weight" count is requested, the flight attendant must obtain a count of all children (12 years of age and younger) who are occupying individual seats.

Although the range of in-flight services varies with the airline and the time of day and length of the flight, the service always involves working from a galley, in most cases with other flight attendants using galley and service equipment and employing a great deal of organization and efficiency. The services are supposed to be presented in a gracious manner, whether they involve arranging trays of beverages, cooking in the galley ovens, or cleaning up afterward. All duties are to be accomplished in an allotted time, with passenger load, weather and many other circumstances to be considered and overcome.

No matter how difficult a particular flight may become, the flight attendant's duty is to remain a confident and reassuring presence. For countless passengers, it is the flight attendant who weighs most in the balance and makes flying pleasurable.

CHAPTER 2

The Flight Attendant's World

As noted, flying is more popular today than ever before. Forces behind this popularity include:

Lower ticket prices

Greater availability of service

Better airplanes of all sizes

The "Baby Boom" generation

A strong economy

Great expectations

Deregulation of the airline industry in 1978 caused intense competition among carriers for market share, which in turn generated fare slashing to attract riders. An even more potent creature of deregulation was a new service delivery system that permits the airlines to draw ridership from many small towns in which airline service was almost unknown prior to 1980. The extra passengers then make possible big-city/medium-size-city pairings that were not possible before. The industry and the public have benefited.

Providing the customers has been the post-World War II population explosion known as the Baby Boom. A strong economy has provided the wherewithal for travel. And great expectations, both by business and by individuals seeking a full life, have provided the motivation.

Great expectations also provide motivation for flight attendants. Senior flight attendants with the best-paying airlines earn close to $40,000 a year; 25 percent of flight attendants exceed $30,000 a year; and 50 percent earn between $20,000 and $30,000.

One of the most attractive benefits of airline work for many airline employees (in all of the various job functions) is travel privileges. Flight attendants not only fly free on their own airlines but are eligible for greatly reduced air fares on other carriers. Thus, 70 percent of flight attendants take four or more pleasure trips a year; 51 percent take five or more. Popular destinations are the Caribbean, Europe, Hawaii, Mexico and Asia. Vacationing activities include sightseeing, sun/beach, enjoyment of a resort atmosphere (at least 30 percent of flight attendants seek out resorts with casinos), and night life.

Changes of the last 15 or more years have brought flight attendants not only greater earning power and better benefits but a more thoroughly professional image in the eyes of the flying public as well. The term "stewardess" has given way to "flight attendant," and sex, age, marital and other barriers have been removed from the position. Whereas flight attendants once had to be female, single, and under 27 years old, 49 percent of flight attendants in a 1989 Association of Flight Attendants (AFA) survey were age 35 and older (the median age was 34), most were either married or divorced, 43 percent had children, and 14 percent were male. Blacks represented a small but growing percentage of flight attendants. Male flight attendants tended to be single and to be younger, on average, than female flight attendants.

In the AFA study, 55 percent of the flight attendants had worked for their respective airlines for more than a decade, including 33 percent who had accumulated more than 15 years of seniority. Fewer than 25 percent had worked for their carriers for less than five years. Such stability within an employee category indicates a high degree of career satisfaction.

Particulars of the Profession

Other aspects of the profession include:

Pay system. Pay generally (but not always) is determined by a negotiated contract. A guaranteed base pay provides for a set number of flight hours per month. You can fly more if extra trips are available. Flight time is block to block — that is to say, gate to gate: The beginning of the flight is marked by removal of blocks from beneath the wheels of the aircraft; the end comes with placement of blocks beneath them at the arrival gate.

Some carriers offer extra pay for night, overwater, international, holiday and overtime flying, and for language qualifications and lead/senior duty position.

The exception to negotiated pay and work rules is experienced at the non-union carrier. Management sets wages and work rules unilaterally at such an airline.

Credit time. Credit time is paid to compensate for ground time and delays or for unscheduled, non-flying time away from home. It is based on a prorated amount of regular duty pay or on a combination of duty time and actual time. A flight attendant usually is paid for either actual flight time, scheduled time, or credited time, whichever is greater.

Per diem pay (expense money). This is a compensation, at a rate of from $1 to $1.50 an hour, for expenses incurred for each hour away from the home base. This pay is tax free and comes to around $360 to $480 a month, with different pay rates obtaining for domestic and international trips.

Other benefits. These include reduced rates for hotels, rental cars, cruises, etc.; in most cases, credit union membership through your airline; and cut-rate international travel packages for personal travel, available through "interline clubs."

Trip trading. Trip trading is allowed by most airlines. Opportunities to swap trips with other flight attendants give you more flexibility for extended days off by working trips back to back. Certain restrictions may apply, and all trip trading must be approved by crew scheduling.

Vacation. From 14 days after the first year to more than 45 days after 25 years on the job.

Medical benefits. The company-provided package usually involves a $100 to $250 deductible. Once the deductible has been met, 80 percent of the charges is paid by the insurance carrier. Maximum employee annual out-of-pocket expense for medical care can range from $500 to about $1,200. Medical insurance is available for immediate family members through you, as the airline's employee.

Effects of seniority. A flight attendant is subject to two types of seniority. The first is in training class, where either Social Security number or age decides one's rank. The second is in actual airline service, where date of hire (i.e., graduation date from flight attendant training) governs one's seniority position.

Seniority ranking in training is used to select observation trips and flight attendants' first domiciles through a bidding process. Once on the job, you will find that seniority governs many aspects of your career: pay scale; base or domicile assignments; duty position on board the aircraft; days off and vacation time; quality and desirability of monthly trips; temporary assignments; order of recall in the event of a furlough; and training, e.g., for upgrade to senior flight attendant or supervisor. Your seniority will be considered under the headings of your domicile and the entire airline system, with the former affecting such items as work schedules and positions and with the latter determining pay scale, transfers (to other domiciles), and other matters.

Negative factors. Waiting in airports, staying in hotels, and eating meals aboard airplanes and in restaurants are routine for flight attendants. These are the aspects of the job that can become humdrum unless you like being on the go so much that even a meal aboard your plane does not become old hat. For many people, hotels and restaurants are exhilarating; a negative becomes a positive.

Along the same lines, the constant flying takes a flight attendant to many different cities and parts of the nation or of the world. Here, too, is an opportunity for the adventurous. Some layovers are long enough to permit sightseeing, shopping, attending events that you know about ahead of time, or trying out new restaurants. Even airports have some interesting shops. But layovers are not "vacation time" and certainly are not always fun. With working flights before and after the layover, flight attendants more often than not spend the time between stints of work either relaxing or sleeping.

A final negative for those who probably should not even consider becoming a flight attendant is the irregularity of the work schedule. Most flight attendants, however, consider their schedule to be a plus, not a minus, because they get far more time off to spend on their personal and family lives than do most other working people.

There's Competition Out There

Because the airline world as a whole is exciting and the flight attendant position is a sought-after one, the supply of flight attendant jobs has not kept pace with demand: Applicants far outnumber the positions available.

The major and national airlines represented more than 88 percent of all jet

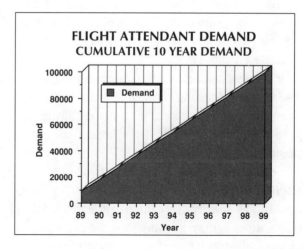

The Flight Attendant's World

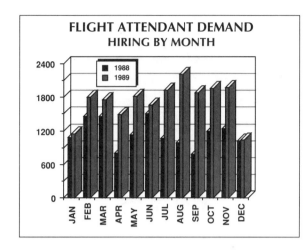

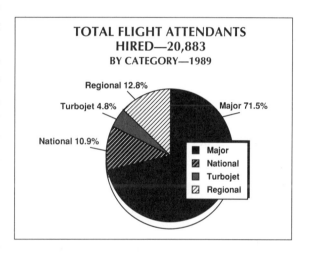

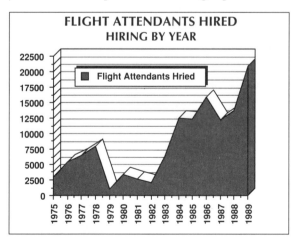

airline hiring as of the end of the 1980s. This airline group will continue to provide the majority of new flight attendant jobs in the foreseeable future. Overall for the industry, Future Aviation Professionals of America (FAPA), an aviation career counseling firm in Atlanta, Ga., has estimated that 10,000 new flight attendants a year will be needed through the year 2000.

But opportunities are widening, and the estimate could fall short of actual need. The integration of smaller airlines into the large-carrier air transport system has brought with it bigger, better and more technically sophisticated aircraft at the small airlines. In turn, these airplanes have made possible the introduction of flight attendants at many of these airlines. The pay is usually less than $20,000 a year, but a commuter or regional airline flight attendant job can be a step toward landing a position with a large carrier. A second attraction of such carriers is rapid advancement.

In some cases, flight attendants with regional airlines might as well be working for a major carrier. For one thing, their airline is owned by the parent company of a major airline. For another, the aircraft flown are high-quality, sophisticated equipment. For the flying public, the main distinction between major carrier and regional airline equipment, other than size, has been jet engines and speed. Now, regional/commuter aircraft offerings include jets, and some of the aircraft are achieving Mach .08 or slightly less, Mach .08* or just a little faster being the maximum speed that aircraft can fly without starting to lose fuel efficiency. Thus, the flying public will perceive regional airline fleets to be on a par with major airline fleets, the sole remaining distinction being size. And even the size of aircraft flown by regional airlines is steadily increasing.

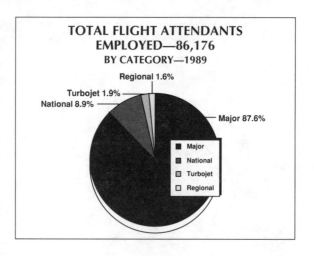

As these airlines become an ever greater presence in the overall air service system, they also will become better employers in terms of salary, benefits and working conditions. And they are quite good now, as the following account shows.

One Flight Attendant's Testimony

I am a flight attendant for a small commuter airline. My duties are similar to those for a larger airline, although our flights are shorter and we serve only beverages. Our longest scheduled flight is one hour, and our shortest is 25 minutes. We do have charter service, and those trips can take us anywhere in the country for up to five days. Our longest charter was 23 days long.

Our fleet consists of four Convair 600 turboprop aircraft that seat 40 or 45 passengers. We have 10 flight attendants in the company. One of these is the Chief Flight Attendant; she does all the hiring and training. One of the things I like about working for a small company is the family-like closeness among employees. Everyone from the president on down is on a first-name basis. Most of the time we are home every night and have

---

* Mach number: a number representing the ratio of the speed of an object to the speed of sound in the surrounding medium (e.g., air) through which the object is moving. The speed of sound in air is roughly 767 miles per hour (at room temperature). Thus, 0.7 Mach number is roughly 537 miles per hour.

Jet Aircraft Orders and Expected Delivery Dates

Airline	Jet Equipment	Orders	Options	Delivery Dates
Alaska	MD-80	19	0	SEP 1990 - MAR 1995
Aloha	B-737-300	4	4	NOV 1992
America West	B-737-300	15	10	1992 - 1995
	B-757-200	10	18	1990 - 1995
American	A-300-600R	6	6	1991 - 1992
	B-757	70	55	JUL 1989 - NOV 1992
	B-767-300	10	30	JUN 1992 - AUG 1993
	MD-80	95	90	1992 - 1996
	MD-11	8	42	1990 - 1991
	F-100	75	75	1991 - 1994
Braniff	B-737	8	0	1990
	A-320	45	50	1990 - 1995
Continental	B-737-300	30	30	1992 - 1995
	A-330/340	20	20	1993-
Delta	B-737-300	50	50	1993-
	B-757-200	17	61	1990 - 1993
	B-767-300ER	9	16	1990 - 2001
	B-767-300	8	4	1990 - 2001
	MD-88	32	72	1990 - 1993
	MD-11	9	31	1991 - 2001
	MD-90	50	110	1994-
Eastern	B-737-300	20	20	1992 - 1995
Midway Airlines	MD-82	29	37	1990 - 1993
	MD-87	3	0	1990
Northwest	A-320-200	23	75	1990 - 1995
	A-330	16	10	JUL 1994 - 1995
	A-340	20	4	1992 - 1995
	B-747-400	11	4	1990 - 1994
	B-757-200	40	40	1993-1998
Pan Am	A-310-300	2	2	APR 1990
Piedmont	B-767-200	3	9	MAR - SEP 1990
Southwest	B-737-300	10	25	1990 - MAR 1991
	B-737-500	20	0	1990 - 1993
TWA	A-330	20	20	1994 - 1996
United	B-737-300	120	130	1989 - 1991
	B-747-400	13	0	1990 - 1991
	B-757	90	60	1990 - 1991
	B-767-300	16	16	1991-1994
USAir	B-737-300/400/500	68	96	1990 - DEC 1992
	B-757	0	10	N/A
	F-100	19	20	1989 - 1990
	MD-82	20	20	SEP 1992 - JUN 1994

Some of the aircraft on current order are intended to replace equipment that has become obsolete or just too old for service. However, many orders are in anticipation of growth. The airlines will be hiring flight attendants for these additions to their fleets.

weekends and holidays off. The majority of our passengers are business people who fly with us regularly. There are quite a few of them who know us by name. My interview was with the Chief Pilot and lasted about an hour. The atmosphere was very relaxed during the entire interview, and within a week I was going through training. My training was one week in ground school and two days in flight training. When I started my flight training, it was in December, and I had flown only once before, in a turboprop airplane. The weather was rough, and you guessed it, I was airsick the entire day. I found out later that two other girls had the same experience, so we all attributed the airsickness to a case of nerves. I was fine the next day. Our airplanes rarely fly above 10,000 feet because of the short flights, and some days, when the weather is bad, we can be right in the thick of it [rain, lightning, sleet, etc.].

A normal day for a flight attendant working in the morning starts with check-in at 6 a.m. Depending on how far you live from the airport, that could mean getting up at 4 o'clock in the morning. Upon check-in, the flight attendant immediately goes out to the airplane and checks emergency equipment, cabin cleanliness, and the catering supplies. It is the flight attendant's responsibility to make coffee and to carry doughnuts, newspapers and a liquor kit out to the airplane. After the coffee is ready, it is poured into two large thermos containers and carried out to the plane.

A morning flight segment consists of seven trips, with the flight attendant finishing up at 2:30 p.m. We start liquor service at 11 a.m. In between flights, we pick up in the cabin, cross seat belts, dispose of the garbage, and order any needed supplies.

We do not have flight attendants on reserve, so about five of my duty days are standby days, and I have to remain home by the phone. Most of the time, they turn into days off because all of us try not to call in sick unless it is absolutely necessary.

In addition to our regularly scheduled flights, we have charter service. One experience I had proved to be quite interesting. A group of businessmen and their wives were going to Arkansas from Detroit with an overnight in St. Louis. On the way down, we had to stop in St. Louis for fuel. The airports in Arkansas got fogged in, and we had to stay on the airplane for two hours in St. Louis. My people decided to start their party early, and my liquor supply diminished in a very short period of time. Trying to act resourceful, I said, "Don't worry, when we get to Arkansas, we'll buy some more." Little did I know that the county in Arkansas where we were to land was dry.

Our passengers expected their party cheer for the trip back to St. Louis. We had to pay someone to drive 20 miles across the county line to buy this awful-looking stuff that was supposed to be Scotch whiskey. Needless to say, my people enjoyed it more because of the manner in which we bought it than for the way it tasted.

We do have meal service on some charter flights. Depending on the group, it can range from a McDonald's meal to a steak dinner. We fly professional hockey, baseball and basketball teams. Since there is only one flight attendant on the airplane, it is not unusual for one of the players to offer to help serve. I have been flying for this airline for two years and have to say this is the most rewarding career a person could have, whether the company you fly for is the largest or the smallest.

The preceding first-person account is reprinted from the October 1981 issue of FAPA's SKYLINE newsletter. The author's name is withheld by request.

A Few Nuts To Munch

A passenger on a typical flight might be assisted by three flight attendants: two females and one male. Among the three of them, they might bring to the job more than 30 years, or 27,000 hours, of experience in safety, training, dedication to their carrier, and service to the public.

How would they pile up so many hours of work?

The work schedule is usually 10 to 17 days a month, with an average of 15 working days. Flight attendants can expect to do from 75 to 100 hours of actual flight time per month, averaging about 85 hours.

Two to 15 trips to the airport are usually made by a flight attendant during a month, with an average of four to five.

Hours on duty (as opposed to flight time) can average from 120 to 200 hours, while hours away from home base will average approximately 240 to 360 per month.

Duty time begins when you report to the crew desk and continues until you are released by the airline after completion of the daily flight schedule. You

Day one: Report at 7:00 a.m.

Flight 1, New York to Miami
8:00 a.m. to 10:30 a.m.
2 hrs./30 min.

Flight 2, Miami to Washington D.C.
12:00 p.m. to 2:00 p.m.
2 hrs.

Day 1 total - 4 hrs./30 min.

Day two: Report at 8:00 a.m.

Flight 1, Washington D.C. to Tampa
9:00 a.m. to 10:50 a.m.
1 hr./50 min.

Flight 2, Tampa to Boston
12:00 p.m. to 2:40 p.m.
2 hrs./40 min.
Day 2 total - 4 hrs./30 min.

Day three: Report at 9:00 a.m.

Flight 1, Boston to New York
1 hr.
Day 3 total - 1 hr.

Time away from base = 52 hours
Using 1 for 3 Trip Rig
Trip Credit equals 52 ÷ 3 = 17 hrs./20 min.

Actual Flight Time Equals   4 hrs./30 min.
                             4 hrs./30 min.
                             1 hr.
                             10 hrs.

Minimum Day Credit = 4 hrs./15 min. per day for 3 days = 12 hrs./45 min.

Duty Rig Credit 1 for 2

Day one-   7:00 a.m. - 2:00 p.m. (7 hrs.) 7 ÷ 2 = 3 ½ hrs.
Day two-   8:00 a.m. - 2:00 p.m. (6 hrs.) 6 ÷ 2 = 3 hrs.
Day three- 9:00 p.m. - 11:00 p.m. (2 hrs.) 2 ÷ 2 = 1 hr.
Total Duty Rig Credit for trip = 7 ½ hrs.

You get paid by whichever method gives you the most pay. In this case you would get paid for 17 ½ hrs.

can expect to be on duty anywhere from six to 18 hours each working day, depending on such variables as weather and mechanical delays. Working time on a flight attendant's duty days averages approximately 10 to 12 hours.

Flight attendants are guaranteed a minimum number of hours free from duty between each trip or group of trips. The length of this rest is determined by the labor contract or the body of company work rules, which takes into account such factors as:

- Number of hours flown.

- Time of day in which the duty period began.

- Distance between the hotel and the airport.

- Next scheduled outbound trip.

- Nature of the flying duty (domestic or international).

For layovers (RON — Remain Overnight, away from home), the company provides travel to the hotel and back to the airport, and it reserves and pays for a hotel room. Flight attendants usually get a discount on food and merchandise at layover hotel stores and restaurants. Other amenities, depending on the company and the union contract, can include dry cleaning and a rental car.

Layovers range from nine hours to two or three days. For domestic flying, the average is 14 hours; for international, 24 hours.

Corporate Flight Attending

The world of flight attending is mostly an airline universe, but corporate fleets also use a few flight attendants.

Corporate flight attending is different in quite a few ways from airline work; it may vary, too, depending on the size of the company and its type and number of aircraft.

There usually are more duties, including menu planning, the buying and preparation of food, cabin cleaning, and restocking of supplies (in effect, a corporate flight attendant may run a small commissary).

In most cases, corporate flight attendants are "on call" and may have to fly at any time. This unpredictable schedule will vary from week to week.

However, with many companies, some of the trips and layovers can be to interesting places for extended periods of time.

Another factor: Your passengers will not be paying customers but, instead, will be corporate executives and company clientele. Thus, getting to know most of your passengers by their names and personal preferences will be a lot easier than if you worked for a commercial airline.

CHAPTER 3

Should You Become a Flight Attendant?

What you want to know at the outset is whether or not flight attending is the right career for you or if you are right for this career.

There are numerous factors to be considered, including whether you believe you would enjoy the kind of life described in the first two chapters.

Other aspects of the job to be considered include:

- Unions.

- The strictness of dress codes and work rules.

- The domicile system, which may well mean that you will have to move to another city in order to accept employment.

- The implications of seniority for such conditions of your employment as "bids" on "lines of flying"; "reserve" or "line holder" status; scheduling flexibility; and jumpseat privileges.

- Considerable technical knowledge that must be mastered.

- And such complications of the job as adverse weather conditions, the wide variety of passenger needs that must be met by a flight attendant, and the range of in-flight emergencies that can arise.

The Unions

The majority of flight attendants in the United States are represented by unions. Delta Air Lines, Continental Airlines, AmericaWest Airlines and Midway Airlines were the only four large carriers whose flight attendants were not represented by a union as of mid-1989.

A union's job is to negotiate contracts for pay, working conditions, and benefits for the flight attendants employed by a given company. Contracts are amendable every one to three years or at any time on agreement by both sides. Flight attendant unions include:

AFA — Association of Flight Attendants

AFL-CIO — American Federation of Labor-Congress of Industrial Organizations

APFA — Association of Professional Flight Attendants

IBT — International Brotherhood of Teamsters

IFFA — Independent Federation of Flight Attendants

IUFA — Independent Union of Flight Attendants

TWU — Transport Workers Union

UFA — Union of Flight Attendants

Local Service Employees Union

At most companies you will be required to join the union after your probation period is over. Some companies require that a flight attendant join the union on the date of hire.

Unions require monthly dues, which usually are payroll-deductible. The dues ranged from $23 to $38 a month as of 1989, depending on the union. These amounts, of course, are subject to change each time the contract is amended.

Dress Codes and Work Rules

From the time you check in to work a trip to the time when you are released from duty, you will be expected to remain in full uniform. The uniform must be clean and in good condition, and company-issued wings or insignia must be fastened to the appropriate garment. This does not mean that you will have to wear the same drab outfit day after day; major airlines have employee uniforms created by leading fashion designers with many practical, durable mix-and-match components so that you can fit your uniform to your own physical type, personality, and taste. Although in many instances you must purchase your first uniform, all replacement items are furnished by the company throughout your career. And the uniform will be redesigned every four to six years.

Punctuality and reliability are paramount qualities. A missed trip can be reason for immediate dismissal from employment. You will be expected to follow all work rules cheerfully and creatively. The difference between an individual who succeeds in making a career of flight attending and one who does not may often be that one follows rules by rote, hiding inner resentment (perhaps even suppressing it), while the other accepts the rules cheerfully and matter-of-factly, seeing in them no constraints to personal and professional effectiveness.

The Domicile System

A domicile is a geographic location chosen by the company for the basing of flight attendants and pilots. The terms "domicile," "base" and "base station" are synonymous. Domiciles can be junior or senior, depending on such matters as where the senior flight attendants wish to be stationed, the size of the base, and the number of scheduled flights to and from the station. As a rule, flight attendants are domiciled at a company's main hubs of operation, which usually are at strategically chosen regional sites, mainly in larger cities.

The system means that you will have no guarantee of being based at a city of your choice. Some airlines require six to 12 months at the first base station before a transfer is permitted. Since you also may be on reserve status from six months to five or more years (depending on many variables), you almost certainly will have to move to the city of your domicile. Reserve status means that you will be "on call" 24 hours a day during duty periods and can be called out at any time. Under such conditions, commuting from a substantial distance will be virtually out of the question.

If you will grow homesick in a strange city, or if you have difficulty adjusting to new environments, flight attending is not the job for you.

Aspects of Seniority

One aspect of seniority is the effect it has on the bid system, or monthly bid-lines.

A schedule of all trips operating from a domicile within a one-month period is issued to all of the flight attendants there. After receiving this schedule, the flight attendants "bid" on the "lines-of-flying" which they prefer. Bid lines for any given month usually are distributed during the preceding month and are awarded three to four days after the "closing date" for bids, which varies from the 10th to the 25th of each month, depending on the airline. The number of bid lines available is determined by the size of the base (domicile) and the level of flying activity.

Seniority determines who gets what trips in these monthly bidding exercises. The terms "line holder" and "reserve" come into play. If a flight attendant is a "line holder" (or "block holder"), the flight attendant "holds a line of time" (has a predetermined schedule) and will know ahead of time, for the entire month, which trips to count on flying. By contrast, a flight attendant on reserve will be on call a certain number of days a month, with the remainder being days off. Reserve or line holder status is determined by seniority and by your ability to bid for and be awarded this status.

Only those with line holder status are awarded specific trips or "lines of time." The trips for the group of line holders are planned in various sequences to allow days off, rest periods, and trips adding up to the required number of both duty hours and rest periods (with rests of appropriate duration) for each line holder.

Usually, around 20 percent of the flight attendants at a base are assigned reserve status. These individuals form a pool of flight attendants on standby to fill in as needed when senior flight attendants are on vacation, leave of absence, or sick leave or when senior flight attendants are delayed by weather or mechanical problems. Reserve can be ready reserve or regular reserve. Ready reserve means getting ready and waiting at the airport in case you are needed for a flight. Regular reserve means that you wait at home or, with some companies, carry a beeper around with you in order to respond to a call for your services on a flight. Depending on the company, bidding usually determines whether a reserve flight attendant is on ready or regular reserve.

The term "on call" means being available to accept a trip on very short notice, i.e., able to report at the airport within one to two hours after telephone notification from the crew scheduling department that you are needed.

Obviously, all of the foregoing factors affect your scheduling flexibility. The more senior you are, the greater your ability to bid successfully for flexible scheduling.

Jumpseat privileges also are affected by seniority. A jumpseat is a seat designated for use by extra flight attendants or by the company's other employees when they are travelling on a company or a business pass. Most airlines have jumpseat privileges.

Generally, these privileges are used either for personal trips or for "deadheading," i.e., catching a ride back to domicile when you do not have an on-duty trip back scheduled.

Theoretically, riding the jumpseat can allow a flight attendant to live in one city and fly out of another. However, the drawback is that jumpseats are assigned on a seniority/first-come, first-served basis. If you miss a trip because you could not get a jumpseat to your domicile, disciplinary action may be taken, including dismissal. For a new flight attendant, therefore, riding the jumpseat to domicile is not a viable option. The risk of being bumped in favor of a more senior employee is simply too great.

Technical Knowledge

You will need to know some fundamentals of aerodynamics and must be able to explain to a passenger what is going on at any given moment. Some passengers require a lot of reassuring, and their fears cannot be dispelled without knowledge. Then, too, in an emergency, the pilot crew sometimes has to rely on information from a flight attendant, e.g., a report on whether or not an engine appears to have been lost based on a visual inspection through a cabin window.

You will need to know time zones, air transport terminology, and the codes of airports, cities and airlines.

Other technical knowledge involves the various kinds of equipment on board the aircraft having to do with safety of passengers.

Complications of the Job

These include adverse weather conditions, a wide variety of passenger needs that must be met by flight attendants, and the range of in-flight emergencies that can arise.

Inclement weather can cause flight delays and airport congestion, bumpy flights, and frightened passengers; in a worst-case scenario, it can lead to an emergency landing or a crash.

Passenger needs range from comforting to assuage fear of flying, to assistance in boarding and performing other acts (in the case of handicapped passengers), to treatment for illness or injury, with an unimaginable array of needs within this range. Then there are other "needs": Some passengers seem to require more attention than others; some wish to be left alone. A flight attendant has to have great social sensitivity to be able to respond to all of these situations.

Emergencies are almost as various as "needs": They include illnesses, injuries, a woman going into labor, drunken or drug-induced misbehavior, individuals attempting to commit suicide (and take everybody else on board along), forced landings because of engine failure or some other impairment – an endless list of possibilities. Flight attendants also have to deal with trying non-emergency situations, such as diversion of the flight to an alternate airport not bedeviled by a snowstorm and the concomitant headaches of trying to calm passengers and to deal with the logistics of getting passengers from the alternate airport either to their destinations or to connecting flights.

You must have a calm, self-confident temperament to handle all of these situations.

What the Airline Wants

The airline is looking for an individual with:

- Poise.

- An attractive, neat appearance.

- Maturity.

- Sensitivity and considerable interpersonal skills.

- Enthusiasm and good attitude.

- Responsibility.
- Awareness.
- Intelligence.
- Friendliness and sociability.
- An adequate general education (some college study is preferred).
- The ability to communicate well.
- And an excellent work history.

It wants to know about:

- Your motivation and aptitude for public contact work.
- Your energy level.
- Your initiative.
- Your work standards.
- Your adaptability.

Admittedly, these add up to a lot of "wants." The airline "wants" a dependable, personable, intelligent, energetic, responsible, people-oriented, caring flight attendant.

Ideally, flight attendants are warm, friendly and outgoing; they sincerely enjoy meeting and helping people. They are independent and can be flexible, for they most likely will be living away from home and family and must be able to adapt to changes in lifestyle, including the new mobility they will experience. Maturity is a key factor: Flight attendants must be able to get along with their co-workers and to handle various situations with passengers. The latter includes accepting both criticism and flattery in a professional manner. A positive attitude, an even disposition, and a ready smile can help smooth the most troubled waters.

The airline profile for a flight attendant also involves physical parameters, as well as age and educational level. The minimum age range is 18 to 21 years old. A chart accompanying this chapter gives minimum age, height-weight parameters, vision requirements, minimum education, and foreign language requirements for nine large airlines.

HIRING QUALIFICATIONS FOR EACH MAJOR AIRLINE

Minimum requirements for application.

Company Name	Minimum Age/yrs.	Height Weight	Vision Minimum	Minimum Education	Foreign Language
American	20	F - 62" - 72" <u>118 lbs. - 157 lbs.</u> M - 62" - 72" 130 lbs. - 180 lbs.	20/50 correctable	high school	helpful
Continental	20	F - min - 62" <u>proportion</u> M - min - 62" proportion	20/20 corrected	high school	helpful
Delta	20	F - to 72" <u>proportion</u> M - to 72" proportion	20/20 corrected	high school	helpful
Eastern	19	F - 61" - 74" <u>113 lbs. - 165 lbs.</u> M - 61" - 74" 140 lbs. - 207 lbs.	20/40 correctable	high school	helpful
Northwest	21	F - min - 62" <u>proportion</u> M - min - 62" proportion	20/20 corrected	high school	helpful
Pan Am	20	F - min - 62" <u>proportion</u> M - min - 62" proportion	20/40 correctable	high school	helpful
TWA	18	F - 62" - 72" <u>113 lbs. - 154 lbs.</u> M - 62" - 72" 127 lbs. - 190 lbs.	20/50 correctable	high school	helpful
United	21	F - 62" - 72" <u>Max. - 159 lbs.</u> M - 62" - 72" max. - 184 lbs.	20/30 correctable	high school	helpful
USAir	21	F - 62" - 72" <u>max. - 169 lbs.</u> M - 62" - 75" max. - 220 lbs.	20/30 correctable	high school	helpful

Should You Become a Flight Attendant?

Maximum Weight by Height			
Southwest Airlines Height	Male max. weight	Female max. weight	
5'2"	130	110	
5'3"	135	115	
5'4"	140	120	
5'5"	145	124	
5'6"	150	128	
5'7"	155	132	
5'8"	160	136	
5'9"	165	140	
5'10"	170	144	
5'11"	175	148	
6'0"	180	152	
6'1"	185	156	
6'2"	190	160	
6'3"	195	164	
6'4"	200	168	
Eastern Airlines Height	Male max. weight	Female max. weight	
5'2"	131	115	
5'3"	136	119	
5'4"	141	123	
5'5"	146	127	
5'6"	151	131	
5'7"	156	135	
5'8"	161	140	
5'9"	166	145	
5'10"	171	149	
5'11"	176	153	
6'0"	181	157	
6'1"	186	161	
6'2"	191	165	

Each airline sets its own standards. These are typical.

CHAPTER 4

The Job Market Today

Essentially, there are six job markets for flight attending:

1. Major airlines

2. National airlines

3. Turbojet airlines

4. Commuter/regional airlines

5. Charter flying with a variety of types of companies (fixed-based operators, small airlines, turbojet airlines that specialize in charter work, corporations)

6. Corporate flying

As noted, the vast majority of flight attendants work for major and national airlines, and these large air carriers will continue to provide most of the flight attending opportunities. But opportunities are expanding continually, even if slowly.

There are other ways to look at the market (for instance, domestic vs. international flying); however, the listing suggested above probably is most useful.

If so, what employers go by what designation?

American, Continental, Delta, Northwest, Pan Am, TWA, United and USAir are examples of major airlines. These airlines all have annual revenues in excess of $1 billion a year.

Air Wisconsin, Alaska, American Trans Air, Midway, Horizon and WestAir are among the national airlines.

Air America, Airlift International, Aspen, Emerald, Express One, Tower and Midwest Express are some examples of turbojet airlines.

Air Midwest, Atlantic Southeast Airlines, Bar Harbor, Business Express, Comair, Command, Mesaba, Metroflight, Pan Am Express, Express Airlines I, Rocky Mountain, Simmons and SkyWest are a few of the regional airlines.

Although there are many companies that fly charters, they comprise a very small market for flight attendant jobs. The same is true of corporate aviation. Your attention should be concentrated on the scheduled airlines: major, national, turbojet and regional.

In planning your career, you will be interested in salary, benefits, locations of each airline's domiciles, the size and stability of the company, and your opportunity for advancement. The image of the airline in the eyes of the travelling public will be important to you, as it will affect your self-image once you are on the job and, in the long run, could affect your employer's chances of survival. You might also be interested in where an airline flies to; for example, does it do any international or overseas flying? To what points in the United States does it fly?

At the end of the chapter are charts from Future Aviation Professionals of America (FAPA) showing flight attendant pay schedules and related information for several airlines in each of the four categories and other FAPA charts showing flight attendant bases for the same airlines.

An Ever-Changing Market

Bear in mind that the airline industry is an ever-changing one and that rankings of airlines are not stable. An airline may drop from the level of a major to a national; move up from a national ranking to a major one; or be swallowed by another airline. The same is true for the smaller airlines; they move up, move down, move into the grasp of other airlines.

Major/Regional Relationships

Major	Network	Regionals
American	American Eagle	Chaparral Command Executive Air Charter Metroflight Nashville Eagle, Inc. Simmons Airlines Wings West
Continental	Continental Express	Bar Harbor Britt Rocky Mountain Airways Southern Jersey
Delta	Delta Connection	ASA Business Express Comair Skywest
Eastern	Eastern Express	Bar Harbor Eastern Metro Express Southern Jersey
Midway	Midway Connection	Iowa Airways Midway Commuter
Northwest	Northwest Airlink	Northwest Airlink (Big Sky) Mesaba Express I Precision
Pan Am		Pan Am Express Resort Commuter
TWA		Air Midwest Metro Airlines Northeast Pocono Airlines TWExpress (MO)
United	United Express	Air Wisconsin Aspen NPA Presidential WestAir Airlines
USAir	USAir Express	Allegheny Commuter Airlines, Inc. CCAir Chautauqua Crown Henson Jetstream Pennsylvania

There are career implications to be considered here: If you take a job with an unstable carrier and it goes out of business, you have to start over. On the other hand, if you take a job with a regional airline that is acquired by a major one, you may or may not "make the grade" with the major carrier. If you do, your job status will have undergone a decided improvement. If you do not, you may have to start your career over. (Some airlines may offer jobs in other positions to flight attendants of an acquired carrier who do not fit the mold of their flight attendants, but, in effect, a shift to another type of job would be starting your career anew.)

Pay special attention, therefore, to the stability of any potential employer. Stability includes profitability and debt structure, labor relations, and the carrier's prospects for survival in its present form in its market niche.

Delta or American would be an example of a highly stable, profitable major carrier. Alaska and Midway are strong, profitable national carriers. Such facts are good knowledge to have even if you are considering employment with another airline. For example, when evaluating a regional or turbojet airline, you should pay attention to its relationships with other airlines. Is it a code-sharing partner with a strong major airline, as ASA is with Delta or Metroflight is with American? Is it owned by a major or national carrier's parent company, as Simmons is by American or Horizon is by Alaska? In such cases, the strength of the major airline partner or sister company will go a long way toward defining the strength of the regional airline.

Obviously, an ASA, paired with powerful Delta, would be more likely to offer stable employment than would a regional carrier struggling to find a profitable niche or wearing out its resources trying to provide traffic feed to a shaky major or national airline. And the regional airline employment with the best prospects for longevity most likely would be with a carrier owned by the holding company of a profitable major airline.

In brief, part of your task in sizing up the job market is to learn which airlines have the best prospects for longevity or for being acquired by some other airline with market strength and a strong balance sheet. Then, of the airlines showing the greatest health, you should begin selecting possible employers from among those with the best reputations as good places to work. Even salary and benefits may take a back seat to such considerations if you are looking for a real career.

"Why?" you might ask. Simple: When an airline is under duress, either from financial instability or because it has labor or image problems, its employees tend to develop a siege mentality. They band together, all right, and develop an esprit de corps in many cases; but the atmosphere is "us against the world," and the situation is stressful. Your career can be warped and cut short by such stress.

The worst of all scenarios occurs when an airline suffers financial travail, labor unrest, and image problems all at the same time. The job stress and emotional turmoil can drive you out of the airline business altogether.

The Union Role

Union representation usually makes for a more stable and better-paid work environment, but occasionally a negative factor comes into play: When the advent of unions drives a wedge between management and labor, both sides develop an adversarial attitude, and the result can be an airline that will not survive.

Do a little advance intelligence work to learn how well union and management get along before deciding to accept a position. The longer an airline has been unionized, the more likely it is to have stable relations between management and the unions that represent its various work groups (pilots, mechanics, flight attendants, etc.). So one of the simplest questions to ask is, "How long has this airline had its unions?" Your intelligence work should not end with this one question, however.

Other questions to ask:

- What is the reputation of the airline's top management in labor relations?

- Does this company have a history of conflict with its unions?

- Have any unions singled this airline out as a target of hard-line union bargaining and other activity in order to make a point?

- Does anyone know of a campaign by unions or by a union to discredit the airline?

- Have union members taken their grievances against the airline to the FAA in the form of reports of improper maintenance or other faulty procedures?

- What is the tone of the union chapters' internal newsletters at the airline? Friendly toward airline management? Subtly critical? Sniping? Abrasive?

Dynamism of the Market

It would be hard to find an industry more volatile and dynamic than the airline business. This is a rapidly growing industry, but with its members

Attending Your Future

Whoever you fly with, if you intend to make a full career of flight attending, you should check up on the company retirement plan.

Employee pension/retirement plans often make up the major portion of a person's retirement income. This situation comes about because some employees fail to take any steps on their own to assure that they will not face straitened circumstances in retirement. In some cases, there is no great harm done: The company has a fine pension/retirement plan, and the employee is taken care of quite well.

Suppose, however, the company for which you work does not have a first-rate employee retirement plan? If your company's retirement program is not first-class, you need to be aware of its deficiencies and make up for these with a supplementary private plan.

Eight of the major airlines offer a dual retirement program consisting of an "A" fund, or defined benefit plan, which promises an employee a specific monthly payout upon retirement, and a "B" fund, or defined contribution plan, to which the company contributes a specific percentage of the employee's salary each pay day.

Among national, turbojet and regional airlines, profit sharing, stock purchases and 401(k) plans are popular vehicles for either the sole retirement plan or for the "B" plan.

Most of the major airline "A" fund programs are calculated using both the employee's number of years of service to the company and the final average earnings (FAE), usually determined by selecting an employee's highest average wages during any consecutive 36 calendar months occurring within the last 120 months (10 years) preceding the date of retirement. For example, United's formula is two percent of the FAE times the number of years an employee has worked for the company.

Most airlines also have a "B" fund retirement plan that involves company contributions or, in a few cases, profit sharing. United's "B" fund is a savings/investment plan to which United contributes nine percent of the flight attendant's annual compensation. Like many "B" fund plans, United's allows you to add up to 10 percent of your annual compensation to the plan and have this money placed in a variety of investment funds. This aspect of the "B" fund could be beneficial to those flight attendants who have difficulty saving money.

Upon retirement, the employee usually receives a monthly allocation from the "A" fund retirement pay and is denied access to the entire amount at once. Eight of 12 "B" fund programs, however, allow you to receive your retirement money in one lump sum, which may be reinvested in a private retirement program. Most retirees roll over their lump sum payments into another retirement program; this way, they are taxed only on the amounts they withdraw for monthly living expenses rather than on the entire lump sum.

Airlines that offer profit sharing as all or part of the retirement program are Continental, Delta, and Southwest. The limitation to such programs is that if the company is not profitable, there is no retirement money. Continental's September 1988 institution of an "A" fund plan was a recognition that its profit-sharing plan could not carry the retirement load by itself. American has a profit-sharing plan that is used as part of an incentive program; the profit sharing does not replace American's "A" and "B" fund retirement programs but is an "extra." Delta's profit-sharing plan, inaugurated in 1989, replaced the defined contribution plan, with Delta's "A" fund remaining unchanged.

---

constantly changing places in terms of market share, sheer size, annual revenue, profitability, and other factors.

How do you gauge the size of an airline? There are several indicators: Among the more obvious are annual revenue, number of employees, fleet size, size and location of hubs (as well as the role the airline plays at the hubs), passengers carried, and number of destinations. Major airlines employ tens of thousands of people; a regional airline may employ as few as 150 and still be large enough to have a few departures with flight attendant service. Naturally, the very small airlines offer little opportunity for you as a flight attendant; yet some rather large regionals present you with the combination of true jet flying in stand-up cabins, a stable and profitable airline, and the possibility of rapid advancement.

Some "regionals" have grown so large that they actually rank today as "national" airlines, according to the Department of Transportation (DOT) definition. That is, they have more than $100 million in annual revenue. Among these, such airlines as Air Wisconsin (based at Appleton, Wis.) and Horizon Air (based at Seattle, Wash.) fly turbojet aircraft with full-service lines of flight. And more and more regional airlines are both growing in size and adding jetliners to their fleets. In addition, some of the advanced turboprop aircraft flown by regional airlines are true airliners; a few of these, such as the Fokker 50 and the ATR 72, are larger than aircraft flown by major airlines back in the mid-1940s. Size is relative, and the modern turboprop airliner is a far more sophisticated, faster, and much safer airplane than were the aircraft flown by the majors four decades ago. More importantly, they are just as "high-tech" and just as luxurious and safe as larger jet aircraft of today.

Only the majors and one or two national and turbojet airlines, however, fly jumbo jets to foreign ports of call. If one of your goals is to visit places that most Americans never have a chance to see, you will want to target one of the few carriers that goes where you want to go.

Aside from the types of aircraft, numbers of each type, and total number of aircraft, you also should know something about the age of an airline's fleet. If an airline has an old fleet, that is a strike against it. A new fleet is a plus.

Benefits and Privileges

Final considerations are such factors as benefits, privileges and pay. The majority of airlines offer benefits packages of some kind, but the larger carriers can afford better ones than can the smaller airlines. The same is true of such extras as jumpseat and pass privileges; you get better value with the larger carriers.

1. *Medical & Dental Coverage.* Most airlines offer excellent medical and dental protection for you and your family. The medical and dental plans are paid for by the company and will cover 80 to 100 percent of the costs, with most providing a maximum out-of-pocket expense for the flight attendant of anywhere from $500 to $1,200 each year. This eliminates the risk of catastrophic losses due to illness or injury.

2. *Retirement.* All major airlines and many lesser ones offer retirement programs, with the bigger companies offering both a company retirement plan and a voluntary plan, usually a 401(k) with various fund programs in which you can invest your money. For company retirement plans, see the sidebar, "Attending Your Future."

A 401(k) program, which most airlines offer, is a tax-deferred retirement plan in which the employee contributes to a fund. In a 401(k), you contribute a percentage of your salary to the fund; your employer is not required to, but generally will either match your contribution or put up a percentage for each dollar you contribute to your account. The maximum contribution is determined by Internal Revenue Service (IRS) regulations.

You have various investment options when participating in a 401(k) plan. Among these are keeping the funds in a savings account and making investments, which may include both conservative and high-risk investment vehicles. The interest earned and payoffs are determined by the type of investment that you make.

The vestment period is determined by the plan the company agrees to: A fund can be fully vested immediately or after as many as seven years. If you choose to leave the company before the fund is vested, you are entitled to withdraw all the money you have contributed to the fund, but no more, and the employer's contribution, if any, goes back to the company. If you withdraw the money after the vestment date, all of the money belongs to you. Your contributions are not taxed until your retirement, or until you withdraw the money prior to retirement.

3. *Profit Sharing.* Profit-sharing options vary from airline to airline and are not available at some of them. However, profit-sharing plans at such major carriers as American, Continental and TWA are potentially a significant bonus to a flight attendant's income, depending on the airline's profit picture.

In the following pages are some FAPA charts showing pass privileges at a number of airlines.

Salary Survey

ALL AIRLINE AVERAGES

Airline	Starting monthly pay in dollars	2nd year maximum monthly pay	5th year maximum monthly pay	Senior flight attendant pay	Flight hours per month minimum/maximum	Expense pay hourly
Major Airline Average	1,027 / 1,297	1,097 / 1,428	1,304 / 1,772	2,185 / 2,814	63 / 86	$1.42
National Airline Average	1,006 / 1,204	1,078 / 1,386	1,365 / 1,654	1,749 / 2,311	70 / 86	$1.29
Turbojet Airline Average	966 / 1,403	1,177 / 1,513	1,382 / 1,756	1,502 / 2,078	63 / 81	$1.25
Regional Airline Average	895	1,092	1,301	1,407	75	$1.00

MAJOR AIRLINE FLIGHT ATTENDANT BASES

Airline	Atlanta, GA	Boston, MA	Chicago, IL	Cincinnati, OH	Cleveland, OH	Dallas, TX	Denver, CO	Detroit, MI	Honolulu, HI	Houston, TX	London, England	Los Angeles, CA	Memphis, TN	Miami, FL	Minneapolis, MN	Nashville, TN	Newark, NJ	New Orleans, LA	New York, NY	Philadelphia, PA	Phoenix, AZ	Pittsburgh, PA	Portland, OR	Raleigh-Durham, NC	Salt Lake City, UT	San Diego, CA	San Francisco, CA	San Juan, PR	Seattle, WA	St. Louis, MO	Washington, DC
American		•	•		•							•		•					•					•		•	•	•			•
America West																					•										
Continental					•		•			•		•					•														
Delta	•	•	•	•		•		•				•		•			•		•				•		•				•		
Eastern	•													•					•												•
Northwest		•	•					•					•		•		•												•		
Pan Am											•	•		•					•												•
Southwest						•				•											•										
TWA												•							•											•	
United			•	•		•	•					•							•								•		•		•
USAir		•										•								•		•				•	•				•

NATIONAL AIRLINE FLIGHT ATTENDANT BASES

Airline	ANCHORAGE, AK	APPLETON, WI	BOISE, ID	BOSTON	CHICAGO, IL	DALLAS, TX	DETROIT, MI	FRESNO, CA	FT. LAUDERDALE, FL	FT. WAYNE, IN	HONOLULU	INDIANAPOLIS	KANSAS CITY, MO	LAS VEGAS, NV	LONG BEACH, CA	LOS ANGELES, CA	MOLINE, IL	NEW YORK, NY	ORLANDO, FL	PHILADELPHIA, PA	PHOENIX, AZ	PORTLAND, OR	RICHMOND, VA	SAN FRANCISCO, CA	SEATTLE, WA	Airline
Air Wisconsin		●								●							●					●				Air Wisconsin
Alaska																●									●	Alaska
Aloha											●															Aloha
American Trans Air				●	●	●	●					●		●				●								American Trans Air
Braniff						●			●				●					●								Braniff
Hawaiian											●					●					●			●	●	Hawaiian
Horizon			●																			●				Horizon
Mark Air	●																									Mark Air
Midway					●															●						Midway
Westair/United Express								●								●								●		Westair/United Express

TURBOJET AIRLINE FLIGHT ATTENDANT BASES

Airline	ATLANTA, GA	ATLANTIC CITY, NJ	BOSTON, MA	CHICAGO, IL	DALLAS, TX	DENVER, CO	DETROIT, MI	LAS VEGAS, NV	LOS ANGELES	MIAMI, FL	MILWAUKEE, WI	MINNEAPOLIS, MN	NEW YORK, NY	ORLANDO, FL	PHILADELPHIA, PA	TEL AVIV, ISRAEL	WASHINGTON, DC	Airline
Air America							●											Air America
Airlift Int'l.										●								Airlift Int'l.
Aspen Airways						●												Aspen Airways
Atlantic			●	●						●				●				Atlantic
Emerald Air		●																Emerald Air
Express One				●										●				Express One
Independent Air	●																	Independent Air
Key								●	●				●					Key
Midwest Express											●							Midwest Express
North American												●						North American
Presidential																	●	Presidential
Rich Int'l.										●								Rich Int'l.
Sun Country												●						Sun Country
Tower Air										●			●			●		Tower Air
Trans Continental													●					Trans Continental
Transocean			●	●									●	●				Transocean
Trump Shuttle			●										●				●	Trump Shuttle

REGIONAL AIRLINE

Airline	AKRON, OH	ALBANY, NY	ALLENTOWN, PA	ATLANTA, GA	ATLANTIC CITY, NJ	BANGOR, ME	BOSTON, MA	BRIDGEPORT, CT	CHICAGO, IL	CINCINNATI, OH	DALLAS, TX	DENVER, CO	DETROIT, MI	DUBOIS, PA	FLORENCE, SC	HARRISBURG, PA	HARTFORD, CT	ISLIP (LONG ISLAND), NY	JACKSONVILLE, FL	JAMESTOWN, NY	LANCASTER, PA	LOS ANGELES, CA	MACON, GA	MANCHESTER, NH	MEMPHIS, TN	MIAMI, FL
Air Midwest																										
Atlantic Southeast				●						●													●			
Bar Harbor/Continental Exp.						●																				
Business Express							●	●									●	●						●		
Chautauqua	●																			●						
Comair										●																
Command		●					●																			
Crown														●												
Express I/Northwest Airlink																									●	
Henson															●			●								
Laredo Air				●																						
Mesaba													●													
Metro Airlines Northeast																										
Metroflight											●															
Nashville Eagle																									●	
Pan Am Express																						●				
Pennsylvania																●										
Rocky Mountain												●														
Simmons									●																	
Skywest																										
USAir Express/Allegheny Commuter			●		●											●					●					

FLIGHT ATTENDANT BASES

Airline	MIDDLETOWN, PA	MINNEAPOLIS, MN	NASHVILLE, TN	NEWARK, NJ	NEW BERN, NC	NEW LONDON, CT	NORFOLK, VA	ORLANDO, FL	PALM SPRINGS, CA	PARKERSBURG, WV	PHILADELPHIA, PA	POUGHKEEPSIE, NY	PROVIDENCE, RI	RALEIGH-DURHAM, NC	READING, PA	SALISBURY, MD	SALT LAKE CITY, UT	SCRANTON, PA	S. BURLINGTON, VT	STATE COLLEGE, PA	ST. LOUIS, MO	WASHINGTON, DC	WILLIAMSPORT, PA	YOUNGSTOWN, WV
Air Midwest																					●			
Atlantic Southeast																								
Bar Harbor/Continental Exp.			●																					
Business Express						●																		
Chautauqua																								
Comair								●																
Command											●											●		
Crown										●														●
Express I/Northwest Airlink		●																						
Henson					●	●										●								
Laredo Air																								
Mesaba		●																						
Metro Airlines Northeast																		●						
Metroflight																								
Nashville Eagle			●											●										
Pan Am Express											●	●												
Pennsylvania	●																			●			●	
Rocky Mountain																								
Simmons																								
Skywest									●								●							
USAir Express/Allegheny Commuter															●			●						

Pass Privileges

MAJOR AIRLINES

Airline	Number of employee passes per year	Cost of passes	Jumpseat privilege available?	Parent passes?	Immediate family passes?	Buddy[1] passes?	Reduced rate travel available?
American	Unlimited after 6 mos.	Tax based on mileage	Yes	Yes	Yes	No	Yes
America West	Unlimited date of hire	Free coach $20 1st class round trip	Yes	Yes	Yes	Yes	Yes
Continental	Unlimited date of hire	$5-$50 svc. charge (travel card)	Yes	Yes	Yes	6 per yr.	Yes
Delta	Unlimited after 6 mos.	$16 round trip	No	Yes	Yes	No	Yes
Eastern	Unlimited after 6 mos.	$13 round trip	Yes	Yes	Spouse and children	No	Yes
Northwest	Unlimited after 6 mos.	$20 round trip	Yes	Yes	Yes	No	Yes
Pan Am	Unlimited after 3 mos.	Free	Yes	Yes	Yes	Yes	Yes
Southwest	Unlimited date of hire	Free	No	Yes	Yes	No	Yes
TWA	Unlimited after 6 mos.	Svc. charge	Yes	Yes	Yes	No	Yes
United	Unlimited after 1 yr.	Svc. charge based on mileage	Yes	Yes	Yes	No	Yes
USAir	Unlimited after 3 mos.	$45/yr. employee $105/yr. per family	Yes	Yes	Yes	No	Yes

[1] A buddy pass is a pass for someone other than family.

NATIONAL AIRLINES

Airline	Number of employee passes per year	Cost of passes	Jumpseat privilege available?	Parent passes?	Immediate family passes?	Buddy passes?	Reduced rate travel available?
Air Wisconsin	Unlimited after 4 mos.	Free on-line	Yes	Yes	Yes	No	Yes
Alaska	Unlimited after 1 mo.	$16 coach $48 1st class round trip	Yes	Yes	Yes	No	Yes
Aloha	Unlimited date of hire	Free	Yes	Yes	Yes	After 2 yrs.	Yes
American Trans Air	Unlimited after 3 mos.	Tax svc. charge	Yes	Yes	Yes	Yes	Yes
Braniff	Unlimited after 6 mos.	Free	No	Yes	Yes	Yes	Yes
Hawaiian	Unlimited after 3 mos.	$40 coach round trip	Yes	Yes	Yes	No	Yes
Horizon	Unlimited date of hire	Free	No	Yes	Yes	Yes	Yes
Midway	Unlimited date of hire	Free	Yes	Yes	Yes	After 3 yrs.	Yes
Mark Air	Unlimited after 6 mos.	Free	No	Yes	Yes	No	Yes
Westair/ United Express	Unlimited date of hire	Free	Yes	Yes	Yes	Yes $30 round trip	Yes

TURBOJET AIRLINES

Airline	Number of employee passes per year	Cost of passes	Jumpseat privilege available?	Parent passes?	Immediate family passes?	Buddy passes?	Reduced rate travel available?
Air America	Unlimited after training	Free	Yes	No	No	No	Yes
Airlift Int'l.	Unlimited date of hire	Free	No	Yes	Yes	No	Yes
Aspen	Unlimited date of hire	Free	No	Yes	Yes	Yes	Yes
Atlantic	Unlimited date of hire	Free	No	Yes	No	No	Yes
Emerald	Unlimited date of hire	Free	Yes	Yes	No	No	Yes
Express One	Unlimited date of hire	Free	Yes	Yes	Yes	Yes	Yes
Independent Air	Unlimited date of hire	Free	Yes	No	No	No	Yes
Key	Unlimited after 1 yr.	Free	Yes	Yes	Yes	Yes	Yes
Midwest Express	Unlimited date of hire	Svc. charge	Yes	Yes	Yes	Yes	Yes
North American	Unlimited after 3 mos.	Svc. charge	Yes	Yes	Yes	No	Yes
Presidential Airways	Unlimited date of hire	$35/yr.	No	Yes	Yes	Yes	Yes
Rich Int'l.	2 per yr. after 6 mos.	Free	No	Yes	Yes	Yes	Yes
Sun Country	None	N/A	Yes	N/A	N/A	N/A	No
Tower	Unlimited after 6 mos.	$23 svc. charge per ticket	Yes	Yes	Yes	Yes	Yes
Trans Continental	Unlimited after 6 mos.	Free	Yes	Yes	Yes	No	Yes
Transocean	Unlimited after 2 mos.	Free	Yes	Yes	Yes	Yes	Yes
Trump Shuttle	Unlimited date of hire	Free	Yes	Yes	Yes	Yes	Yes

REGIONAL AIRLINES

Airline	Number of employee passes per year	Cost of passes	Jumpseat privilege available?	Parent passes?	Immediate family passes?	Buddy passes?	Reduced rate travel available?
Air Midwest	Unlimited	Free	No	Yes	Yes	Yes	Yes
Atlantic Southeast	Unlimited	Free	No	Yes	Yes	No	Yes
Bar Harbor/ Continental Expr.	Unlimited	Free	No	Yes	Yes	No	Yes
Business Express	Unlimited	Free	No	Yes	Yes	Yes	Yes
Chautauqua	Unlimited	Free	No	Yes	Yes	No	Yes
Comair	Unlimited	Free	Yes	Yes	Yes	Yes	Yes
Command	Unlimited	Svc. charge	No	Yes	Yes	No	Yes
Crown	Unlimited	$45/yr.	No	Yes	Yes	No	Yes
Express Airlines I/ Northwest Airlink	Unlimited	Free	No	Yes	Yes	Yes	Yes
Henson/ USAir Express	Unlimited	Free	No	Yes	Yes	No	Yes
Laredo Air	Unlimited	Free	Yes	$10/each	$10/each	$10/each	Yes
Mesaba	Unlimited	Free	No	$5/one way	Yes	No	Yes
Metro Airlines Northeast	Unlimited	Free	No	Yes	Yes	Yes	Yes
Metroflight	Unlimited	Free	Yes	Yes	Yes	Yes	Yes
Nashville Eagle	Unlimited	Varies	Yes	Yes	Yes	No	Yes
Pan Am Express	Unlimited date of hire	Free	No	Yes	Yes	No	Yes
Pennsylvania	Unlimited	$45/yr. $15 round trip	No	Yes	No	No	Yes
Rocky Mountain	Unlimited date of hire	Free	No	Yes	Yes	Friend of the month	Yes
Simmons	Unlimited	Svc. charge	No	Yes	Yes	No	Yes
SkyWest	Unlimited	Free	Yes	Yes	Yes	Yes	Yes
USAir Express/ Allegheny Commuter	Unlimited	$45/yr. $15 round trip	No	Yes	Yes	No	Yes

Part II

YOUR JOB SEARCH

CHAPTER 5

Getting Started: Resumes and Letters

Having decided that you want to be a flight attendant and having narrowed down the field of airlines for which you would most like to work, your next step is to know which airlines are hiring and how to get the attention of those individuals who do the hiring.

If you know the right way to read their articles, a good many publications are excellent sources of information about who is hiring. When skimming through most of them, look for stories about particular airlines for which you might like to work. Then try to decide, based on the article, whether the airline is growing or static. If the article paints a picture of a rapid expansion program either underway or about to begin, then you know that this airline either is already hiring a lot of flight attendants or will be doing so very soon.

Sources for information include *Aviation Week & Space Technology*, *The Wall Street Journal*, local newspapers, Janice Barden's Corporate Aviation Agency (for those seeking corporate jobs), FAPA's annual *Flight Attendant Directory of Employers* and FAPA's monthly *Flight Attendant Job Report*. These last two publications specifically target job markets for flight attendants.

Career Pilot magazine also is a good source of information about jobs for flight attendants.

Air Transport World has long been a standard among monthly commercial aviation publications, while a more recent rival is *Airline Executive*; *Commuter Air Magazine* was adopted in 1988 by the Regional Airline Association as a monthly forum; and *Business/Commercial Aviation* has the advantages of experienced staff and coverage of both corporate and airline flying (particularly of the smaller airlines). All of these magazines can prove valuable in keeping you informed about who is expanding, who is cutting back, and who is more likely to be hiring. They also add to your store of information about particular airlines. Most can be found in public or college libraries.

Once you know who is hiring and where you want to apply, you will need current addresses. FAPA's *Flight Attendant Directory of Employers* includes current addresses and recommended contact names. Address changes and new employment information are published in the monthly *Flight Attendant Job Report* newsletter.

There are other sources for obtaining the appropriate company addresses, many of which can be found at the local library. The *World Aviation Directory* (WAD) is the most comprehensive manual; it includes addresses and general information for specific companies. However, the contact names listed in the WAD are not necessarily the ones to use as contacts on employment correspondence sent to the companies. Another good source is the *Airline Industry Directory*. Again, however, some care must be taken about the names used as contacts.

There is nothing to keep you from calling a company and talking with the switchboard operator. Whenever possible, you should ask for a contact name and the title of the person actually responsible for recruitment, along with the address. Without fail, the spelling of the person's name should be verified.

You also can talk with a company's employees.

Be Organized

Your first step is organization. Start a file or job search log to keep an accurate record of which airlines you write requesting applications, of the airlines to which you submit resumes, and of the date of submission. Later, you can use the same system for recording job search updates and company contacts. Retain a copy of each piece of correspondence you have sent to or received from each airline; you may be asked during an interview about information you have sent previously.

A job search log will make it easy for you to keep up with your status with respect to every airline for which you might like to work. A typical file will include news articles about the company, a list of the company's minimum qualifications, copies of complete employment applications, records of updates and revisions, telephone numbers of contacts, and letters of recommendation. Add to the file whatever you feel will be helpful, but do not include irrelevant data. (See page 66 for a sample job search log.)

Request applications from a broad range of airlines. Use a resume package, including a current resume, a cover letter, and a self-addressed, stamped envelope. Send completed applications with cover letters and resumes to a broad range of airlines — at least 10 to 20. Update your files every few months or any time you have a change in qualifications, address, or telephone number. Re-apply every six months to a year with a new application and resume (more frequently if possible).

Network with your friends to find job opportunities. Call and visit prospective employers regularly. Use an answering machine or service to provide 24-hour phone coverage.

One reason you want to stay in touch with so many airlines is that people often "flunk" their first interviews. Learning how to interview well takes practice, so a couple of interviews with companies by which you do not mind being rejected could be very helpful. You do not want your very first interview to be for your "dream job."

Letters Get Results

Your second step is to construct a professional and grammatically correct letter indicating your interest in being employed by XYZ Company and requesting a flight attendant application form. This letter should be addressed to the manager of in-flight services. Include a self-addressed, stamped envelope. Apply to as many companies as you can. If you do not apply, you will not be hired, no matter how many new flight attendants are being added by an airline. Furthermore, having an application on file allows you to update as your qualifications improve.

It may take several weeks to receive a response to your correspondence since the companies are busy handling thousands of inquiries. Be patient. If you do not get a response, try sending a second letter.

Another method of obtaining an application is to pick one up in person. Many airlines have them available at their ticket counters. You may pick these up when you travel, or you could have a friend or relative residing near one of an airline's hubs send the application to you.

Choose the companies that you most want to work for and update with them frequently. Do not limit yourself by being too selective. If a company is hiring, update every month. Update at least every six months. Of course, your update correspondence should restate your desire to work for the company. Include any additional experience you might have gained since your last letter.

With thousands of unrelenting flight attendants flooding personnel offices with reams of job-search correspondence daily, you will need to establish an organized communication program that will make you stand out among the multitude. You need a competitive edge.

Since most incoming mail is handled by clerks who simply shuffle letters from one department to another, a good business letter (one that includes your full name and address and a clear statement of purpose) will get the best results.

Should your records be pulled for review, the letters in your file will give the reader a summary of your professional credentials.

Your correspondence reflects you and your personality. Through your letter, you make an impression, good or bad. From the reader's viewpoint, the letter is you. So be sure that it represents you in a fitting manner.

An important point: Pretentiousness in correspondence is just as offensive as it is in a face-to-face situation. The offense is amplified because the letter is a permanent record glaring at the reader in black and white every time it is read.

Perhaps one of the best ways to evaluate your letter is to ask yourself before placing it inside the envelope, "How would I feel if I received this letter?"

Guidelines for Correspondence

Define the purpose of your letter and state it in the opening paragraph. The beginning is the most important part of your letter, and brevity is vital. Save all the detailed information and lengthy explanations for your application or for your interview. Excessive verbiage not only detracts from the effectiveness of your letter, it wastes time for both you and the reader. The physical appearance of the letter also is very important.

The following guidelines will assist you in improving your job search letters.

1. *Write promptly.* Responding to a situation immediately is essential. Professionals like to deal with people who stay on top of things. This

goes for situations that you glean from your reading as well as for response to correspondence from a company.

2. *Know a name.* Whenever possible, address your correspondence to an individual, including the person's title in the address at the top of your letter. The reader is a VIP (very important person), so whatever you do, do not misspell his or her name.
3. *Type all letters.* Do not handwrite your job search letters. Each letter should be neatly typed and presented in an acceptable business format.
4. *Determine your purpose.* Ask yourself, "Why am I writing this letter?" The answer should be concisely conveyed in the opening paragraph of your letter.
5. *Write as you talk.* Except for refining the grammar, the wording of your letter should be the same as if you were having an opportunity to talk one-on-one with the recipient.
6. *Be economical with words.* Cover your subject as concisely as possible. Do not waste words, but do not sacrifice courtesy, either.
7. *Do not oversell.* Stay clear of being too "me-oriented." Stick with the facts; just present them in your favor.
8. *End positively.* The ending is the second most important part of a letter. Avoid trite closings, such as "Looking forward to hearing from you soon. . . ."
9. *Use good grammar and spelling.* Do your very best to make sure the letter is grammatically perfect. Watch for spelling errors, especially in names of people or companies.
10. *Go easy on the "thank you's."* Do not overdo your gratitude for the reader's time. Use the words "thank you" at appropriate times only. They sound more sincere when used sparingly.
11. *Use good paper.* Use quality paper for your resume and letters. It should be white or cream-colored and should be at least a 25 percent rag-content, opaque bond paper. Most printers have a nice selection to choose from.
12. *Mind your taxes.* Keep adequate records to justify all the expenses you incur (e.g., resumes) in your job search efforts. Consult your tax advisor for details.

Following are two sample query letters. The first is self-guiding, taking you through the letter step by step. The second is ready to mail.

Flight Attendant

The Heading Should Include Your Current Address & Phone Number, Date, Company Address & Salutation

4959 Massachusetts Boulevard
Atlanta, GA 30337
(404) 997-8097

January 1, 1990

FAPA Air
Attn: R.J. Carter, Recruitment
Atlanta Hartsfield Airport
Atlanta, GA 30320

Dear Ms. Carter:

State Your Objective In The Opening Paragraph And Highlight Your Qualifications In The Body Of The Letter

I am interested in career flight attendant employment with FAPA Air and have enclosed a resume for your review. My work experience and qualifications include:

* Over four years public contact work experience as a receptionist, sales clerk and custom interior representative.

* Graduate of college majoring in Political Science/International from the American College of Switzerland in Leysin, Switzerland and the University of Colorado in Boulder, Colorado.

* Current Advanced Lifesaving Certificate from American Red Cross in Boulder, Colorado.

* Beauty and Modeling Course from Glamour Magazine in Stanford, California.

* Private Pilot Course from Friment Flight School in Friment, California.

The Closing Paragraph Should Say Something About You As An Individual And Request Action

My extensive public contact work has reinforced my desire to continue working with people on a daily basis. I am a highly motivated individual with a positive outlook on life. Through my current employment, I often meet people associated with the aviation industry, and I would be proud to be a representative of FAPA Air.

If required, please forward an employment application in the enclosed self-addressed stamped envelope.

I recognize the significant career opportunities available at FAPA Air and look forward to discussing my qualifications with you personally in the near future.

Sincerely,

Willa U. Hireme
Enclosures

1286 Bath Street
Langley, SC 29828
1 (703) 279-3070
December 14, 199-

Acme Airlines
Hartsfield Atlanta International Airport
Atlanta, GA 30320
Attn: R.J. Carter, Flight Attendant Recruiting

Dear Ms. Carter:

I am seeking career employment as a flight attendant with Acme Airlines. My work experience and other qualifications include:

> Three years of experience as a flight attendant under Part 121 in scheduled, charter, domestic and international passenger operations. Qualified on DC-8, DC-10 and A-300 aircraft.
>
> Two years of college in pre-nursing at the University of Maryland, with extensive first-aid training and current CPR certification.
>
> One year of restaurant management experience — responsible for supervision of payroll, purchasing and scheduling.
>
> Five consecutive years of public contact work experience in both the airline and restaurant businesses.
>
> Six years of residency in West Germany, where I learned to speak, read and write German fluently.

I have come to know and enjoy the airline business not only through my experiences as a flight attendant but also as the daughter of an airline captain. My public contact work experience, language skill, and first-aid training fit me for the position of flight attendant. I should be an asset to Acme Airlines.

Please forward an employment application in the enclosed self-addressed, stamped envelope.

Sincerely,

Mary Jones

Your Resume

In order to fare well with potential employers, you must develop a quality resume and cover letter. Since a resume is used as a pre-screening device, it should be included in your first correspondence to a company. One point that should never be forgotten is that every written communication from you to the potential employer should include a cover letter (which can be a spinoff from your letter of inquiry) and your resume. And every application that you submit should be accompanied by both the cover letter and the resume.

You cannot place too much emphasis on the completeness of your resume, which is a history of your educational background and work experience. Since distance often prevents you from communicating directly with airline employment offices, you must correspond to introduce yourself. The resume can help make you materialize before the inner eye of a personnel director or recruiting officer. It may be the most important document you ever prepare.

Do not try to deceive anyone with whom you correspond while seeking employment. Employers are not so unaware of experience situations as many people believe they are, nor do they have time to read insignificant details. Give only the relevant facts and information needed to introduce yourself properly. Though the primary purpose of a resume is to obtain an interview, a well-prepared resume also will provide an important focal point for conversation between the applicant and the prospective employer during a later interview.

Try to keep your resume to one page; never use more than two. Stress points that show you are qualified; do not call attention to deficiencies. Stick to facts; your accomplishments, not your opinions, are important to the employer. Your claims and references may be checked, so misleading information may have a detrimental effect, not only for the moment, but for your career goals.

Proofread your resume and perhaps have someone else check behind you. A second eye may catch flaws you have not noticed. Avoid using long, complex sentences. Organize your thoughts within each paragraph around a single subject. Develop this subject before continuing to the next one, which will be contained in the next paragraph.

List events and past jobs in reverse chronological order, i.e., with the last job or event listed first. Double-check your spelling, word usage, grammar, and the general organization of your resume.

When you are satisfied with the product, have it typeset and reproduced at a printing shop (do not use a copying machine).

Following is a resume checklist that has been effective for flight attendant applicants — but first, a few words of general advice:

Show your objective and work history, followed by your educational background and any additional information that is relevant. Limit your listed work experience to your last three jobs or to those jobs that are pertinent to public contact experience. Then include all other work experience in one short,

RESUME CHECKLIST

RESUME OF:
Show full name, mailing address, phone number.
EMPLOYMENT OBJECTIVE:
Flight attendant (note: Stating a job objective is optional).

EXPERIENCE:
List professional data.
Work experience in reverse chronological order, listing:

- Dates (start/end).

- Names, locations of companies.

- Your job titles, followed by very brief but factual description of your duties.

The format is job by job, with starting and ending dates for each job; name, then location of company for which you worked; then job title and duties. Repeat this form three times.

EDUCATION & SPECIAL TRAINING:
Include college degree and professional schools and/or courses completed that relate to your job objective.

PERSONAL DATA:
General health.
Hobbies.
Foreign languages.
Travel experience.
Volunteer work.

general paragraph that sums up the type of work in which you were involved.

Remember, your objective is to produce a professional, one-page resume. The format and style suggested below will get the best results.

Your resume will be used as a preliminary screening device prior to the distribution of applications. It will be scored; a high-scoring resume can produce an interview opportunity. In fact, some companies often grant an interview from a resume alone.

In summary, your resume should be used:

- To request applications and interviews.

- To accompany completed employment applications.

- To update your files every two to six months.

- As a calling card when you are visiting employment offices without a formal interview scheduled.

- As a convenience to your interviewer, who may ask for a resume during the interview.

- As an update of your qualifications during the interview if anything significant has changed.

Carry extra resumes with you to distribute when you make airline contacts. Resumes make it easier for anyone who knows you to recommend you because he or she can refer to the resume received from you.

Following are three sample resumes.

LAWRENCE DAVIDSON

4959 Massachusetts Boulevard Douglasville, GA 30134	Social Security Number 252-17-0666	Home Telephone (404) 997-8097

OBJECTIVE: Career flight attendant employment.

EMPLOYMENT HISTORY:

BANQUET MANAGER
MAY 88 - Present — Community Center Foundation, Atlanta, GA 31721 — Greet, seat and serve retreat groups and community organizations using the facilities. Organize functions including menu planning and staffing requirements. Supervise dining room and kitchen staff.

SALES AUDIT DEPARTMENT MANAGER
MAY 87 - FEB 89 — The Athlete's Foot, 3735 Atlanta Ind. Pkwy., Atlanta, GA 31721 — Trained all personnel in register and system use. Conducted training seminars for in-field personnel. Extensive travel and customer service experience.

LEAD STORE MANAGER
JUL 85 - DEC 86 — Uptons Dept. Stores, 3565 Austell Road, Marietta, GA 31721 — Supervised men's and boys' departments. Screened, hired and trained 100+ employees. Produced highest sales out of a ten-store system.

MAY 76 - JUL 85 — Continuous full and part-time employment since high school including positions as a sales manager, sales associate, temporary executive assistant, host and public relations liaison at Six Flags over Georgia (recreation park).

EDUCATION:

B.A. DEGREE - JOURNALISM
AUG 78 - DEC 80 — University of Georgia, Athens, GA 31721 — Member: Phi Kappa Psi fraternity, Sigma Delta Chi National Journalism Honor Society; UGA Men's Glee Club. Dean's List. Financed 50% of education through employment.

VOLUNTEER EXPERIENCE:
- JUL 88 - Present — Volunteer: Fellowship of Christian Airline Personnel, Atlanta, GA
- NOV 86 - Present — Fundraiser: High Museum of Art, Atlanta, GA
- FEB 79 - Present — Volunteer: Carnival for Cure (Leukemia Philanthropy), Atlanta, GA

SPECIAL TRAINING:
APR 88 — CPR Certification: American Heart Association, Atlanta, GA

TRAVEL EXPERIENCE: Recreational and professional throughout the United States.

PERSONAL DATA: Born: July 16, 1958; 5'6½", 140 lbs.; Excellent health. Interests: Aerobics, tennis, reading.

AVAILABILITY: **TWO WEEKS NOTICE**

WILLA U. HIREME

Current Address	**Social Security Number**	**Permanent Address**
4959 Massachusetts Boulevard	123-56-8907	64 Spring Lane, Apt. #2
Atlanta, GA 30337		Avondale Estates, GA 30320
(404) 997-8097		(404) 342-9764

OBJECTIVE: Career flight attendant employment.

EMPLOYMENT HISTORY:

MAY 84 - Present

PUBLIC RELATIONS
S & M Builders
123 S. Harriston
Atlanta, GA 31721

Meet and assist home buyers with custom interior selections; Coordinate between buyer and home builder. Seasonal employment.

MAY 82 - MAY 84

RECEPTIONIST / ACCOUNTANT
Friment Airport
Route 270
Friment, CA 21721

Handled typing and filing; Answered phones; Performed bookkeeping and general clerical duties.

SEP 80 - MAY 82

BOOKKEEPER / SALES CLERK
McQuarries Pharmacy
1908 Parkway West
Menlay Park, CA 21721

Assisted customers with services; Controlled cash management. Responsible for inventory and scheduling.

EDUCATION:

AUG 82 - MAY 86

B.S. DEGREE - POLITICAL SCIENCE
Univ. of Colorado
Old Route 1
Boulder, CO 41721

Social Chairman/Member: Delta Gamma Sorority; Ski Team, Intramural Sports Program.

SPECIAL TRAINING:

JUL 85 - Present — Private Pilot Course: Friment Flight School, Friment, CA
APR 82 - MAY 84 — Advanced Lifesaving Certificate: American Red Cross, Boulder, CO
JUN 84 - JUL 84 — Glamour Beauty School: Glamour Magazine, Stanford, CA

VOLUNTEER WORK:

SEP 80 — March of Dimes Fund Raiser Participant: Menlay Park, CA
SEP 80 - AUG 82 — Meals-on-Wheels program delivery person/food server: Menlay Park, CA

LANGUAGE SKILL: Two years of intermediate study of French.

TRAVEL EXPERIENCE: Throughout the United States, Europe and the Middle East.

PERSONAL DATA:
Birthday: April 20, 1964
Height/Weight: 5'3"/105 lbs.
Health: Excellent
Interests: Travel, sports, flying, writing

AVAILABILITY: **TWO WEEKS NOTICE**

SUE ELLEN COMSTOCK

345 Wood Path Crossing	SSN	Home: (602) 456-1876
Brownville, AZ 39283	234-67-0987	Alternate: (602) 457-9081

OBJECTIVE: Career flight attendant employment.

EMPLOYMENT HISTORY:

MAR 88 - Present
OFFICE MANAGER
Farmers Insurance Group
9402 N. Central, Suite 7
Phoenix, AZ 31721

Supervise 6-8 staff members in front office operations hiring and scheduling; write insurance policies for clients; process claims. Extensive public contact. Was promoted from secretary position.

DEC 87 - FEB 88
CUSTOMER SERVICE AGENT
Stateside Airlines
4828 E McDowell
Phoenix, AZ 31721

Graduated from training with honors. Worked at ticket counter handling passenger reservations and ticketing.

SEP 83 - JAN 87
SALES REPRESENTATIVE
Brooks Fashions
9820 A Metro Pkwy.
Phoenix, AZ 31721

Achieved a successful sales record; Performed cashier duties with precision and accuracy. Extensive public contact and customer experience.

Prior to SEP 83

My employment history includes positions as sales representative and cashier.

EDUCATION:

SEP 82 - MAY 84
A.S. DEGREE
Phoenix Comm. Coll.
Phoenix, AZ 31721

Major: Fashion Merchandising.
Dean's List. GPA: 3.8.

Prior to SEP 82

In high school I was an honor roll student and was actively involved as a member of the Student Council. I also served as Junior Achievement Vice President and Girls Track Club Treasurer and was a Homecoming Queen nominee.

SPECIAL TRAINING:
MAR 88

CPR Certification: American Heart Association.

LANGUAGE SKILLS:

Possess a basic conversational knowledge of French.

VOLUNTEER WORK:

Child Caretaker: St. Jeromes Church, Phoenix, AZ
10K Walk-A-Thon: Feed The Hungry 10K, Phoenix, AZ

TRAVEL EXPERIENCE:

Throughout the United States.

PERSONAL DATA:

Born: July 10, 1960
Height: 5'6"
Weight: 105 lbs.
Interests: Swimming, running, collecting miniatures and dancing.

AVAILABILITY:

ONE WEEK NOTICE

The Cover Letter

The cover letter is your personalized statement of your desire to work for a certain company. For the reader picking up your file for the first time, it will give that all-important first impression of you. It will introduce you and highlight your qualifications and experience. It should be brief, stating your objective, requesting action, and expressing your appreciation for the time your reader will take to look over your credentials. A professional, well-constructed cover letter will spark the reader's interest and make him or her want to read your resume.

A cover letter should start with a heading, including your current address and phone number, the date, the company's address, and the salutation (Dear So-and-So:). Each time you use the letter, you should target it to a specific contact at this particular airline company.

The second part of the letter is the body, which will state your objective in the opening paragraph and highlight your qualifications (work experience, education) in the following paragraphs.

Finally, there is the close, in which you need to say something about yourself as an individual and invite action, e.g., an interview. Use the standard "Sincerely" for the complimentary close, followed by your signature, to finish the cover letter.

Again, the rules discussed above with respect to correspondence with a potential employer apply in spades. To review a few of these:

Determine your purpose. Ask yourself, "Why am I writing this letter?" The answer should be concisely conveyed in the opening paragraph of your letter.

Write as you talk. Except for refining the grammar, the wording of your letter should be the same as if you were having an opportunity to talk one-on-one with the recipient.

Be economical with words. Cover your subject as concisely as possible. Do not waste words, but do not sacrifice courtesy, either.

Do not oversell. Stay clear of being too "me-oriented." Stick with the facts; just present them in your favor.

Following is a sample cover letter.

1286 Bath Street
Langley, SC 29828
1 (703) 279-3070
December 14, 199-

Acme Airlines
Hartsfield Atlanta International Airport
Atlanta, GA 30320
Attn: R. J. Carter, Flight Attendant Recruiting
Dear Ms. Carter:

    I am seeking career employment as a flight attendant with Acme Airlines. Enclosed is a resume summarizing my work experience and other qualifications, which include:

> Three years of experience as a flight attendant under Part 121 in scheduled, charter, domestic and international passenger operations. Qualified on DC-8, DC-10 and A-300 aircraft.
>
> Two years of college in pre-nursing at the University of Maryland, with extensive first-aid training and current CPR certification.
>
> One year of restaurant management experience — responsible for supervision of payroll, purchasing and scheduling.
>
> Five consecutive years of public contact work experience in both the airline and restaurant businesses.
>
> Six years of residency in West Germany, where I learned to speak, read and write German fluently.

    I have come to know and enjoy the airline business not only through my experiences as a flight attendant but also as the daughter of an airline captain. My public contact work experience, language skill, and first-aid training fit me for the position of flight attendant. I should be an asset to Acme Airlines.

    Realizing that significant career opportunities are available with Acme Airlines, I look forward to discussing my qualifications with you in person in the near future.

Sincerely,

Mary Jones
Encl.

    You should now be able to develop proficiency in preparing letters and a resume. You are ready to consider the dos and don'ts of the application process.

JOB SEARCH RECORD

COMPANY ADDRESS	REQUESTED APPLICATION SENT RESUME (DATE)	REPLY RECEIVED (DATE)	APPLICATION SENT (DATE)	FOLLOW UP (DATE)	PERSON(S) CONTACTED	REMARKS

CHAPTER 6

The Application Process

Once you have your first airline application in your hand, you are at the commencement of the application process. The process begins when you actually sit down and begin filling out the first form.

Employment applications are graded and reduced to a numerical score by the airlines. They are graded on appearance, content, and completeness. Individual categories, such as work history and experience, are scrutinized carefully.

There is another highly important fact to understand. Applications are legal documents, and all information contained in them is considered to be true. Any misinformation, depending on the situation, can lead to immediate dismissal.

A few preliminaries: When you receive your flight attendant application form, take the time to read it over carefully before taking any action. Then assemble all the items you will need to do the physical job of filling out an application form; also, get together the names, addresses, phone numbers and job titles of your personal references. Make a photocopy of the application form so you can fill out the photocopy first. Thus, if you make any errors, you will not have ruined your original.

The Application Form

Applications follow a when (date), where (company name and address) and what (job description) format. They can be tedious to fill out, and mistakes are inevitable. It is for this reason that you are beginning your work with the photocopied form.

Be patient. Keep your mind focused on your basic objective: to give as professional, positive and appealing an impression of yourself as possible without distorting the truth.

Begin filling out your practice application with your name and present address, as well as your permanent address if it is different (be sure you can be reached through any address that you write down). Use a three-line address, including ZIP codes. Some applications will require phone numbers with area codes. Use the nearest U.S. Post Office and the telephone directory for the addresses and phone numbers of references if you have not gotten these from the references themselves. Note well: Some applications state that if this information is not complete, the application will be discarded.

Keep all entries brief and to the point. In many instances, you will be able to refer to your resume, which you should already have prepared, for the wording of entries.

Position applying for. Your answer here depends on the company. Usually "Flight Attendant" will suffice, but some companies hire "Customer Service Representatives." Be sure you use the right terminology for each company.

Type of work desired. This section should be filled out completely, in a positive tone. Obviously, you desire full-time employment. Include the locations you prefer, but be sure to mark every item which indicates that you are flexible with regard to working hours, shifts, days worked, and locations. Do not eliminate yourself this early in the game by seeming inflexible.

When you can report to work. Applications always ask, "How soon can you report to work following notification?" or other phraseology to the same effect. The preferred answer is "Immediately." Be sure that, if you have a prior commitment, you can be available on the date you give.

Work experience. Be sure to account for your time. Many companies will require you to give the names and addresses of people who can vouch for your activities during periods of self-employment or unemployment.

Unless there are extenuating circumstances or unless you are able to list activities for the period that have an equal footing with a job, unemployment will not reflect favorably. If you were enrolled in college courses or involved in flight training or other professional training during the "unemployed" time, list that you were "in school."

Self-employment sometimes is questioned since there are people who claim self-employment instead of admitting that they were unemployed. Be sure that you can substantiate your claim with business licenses, affidavits, records of your business activities, or whatever documentation that you feel is appropriate.

When filling in the dates of employment, the beginnings and endings usually can be entered as month and year unless the application specifies otherwise.

Read the instructions carefully. Some companies require a history from your 18th birthday to the present or for the past 10 years. Be sure that you provide what the company is requesting.

Language skills. Foreign language skills are not required but will be helpful when you apply to carriers that fly foreign routes. The most preferred languages are Spanish, German, French and Japanese. Having a language skill and using it can bring you higher pay rates.

Travel experience. Travel experience is not required by any airline. It can be helpful, however, and certainly is worth putting on your applications. At the interview, your travel may be the only difference between you and another applicant in the minds of the interviewers.

Asked to resign. Applications do not ask specifically for this information. Rather, they ask your reason for leaving a job. Never be negative in your answer. This is not dishonesty; it is simple self-preservation, which anybody with a sense of belonging on the face of the earth practices. Acceptable answers to this question include "career advancement," "to pursue a flying career," "departmental transfer," "furlough," "Chapter 11 reorganization of employer," "moved away," and "personal; to be discussed."

Many companies want to know why you left each position. Do not eliminate yourself here. All answers should be positive. Such answers as "job dissatisfaction," "disliked employer," "personality conflict," etc., are detrimental since they indicate a possible malcontent personality or an inability to get along with other people.

And never mind that some employers (even in the airline industry) are less than desirable. You cannot count on a concurring judgment about any given employer from the individual reading your application. In itself, an excessive number of employers in a short time may indicate instability to potential employers (though your reasons for going from job to job may have been as good as gold), so be careful how you state your reason for leaving a position.

If you need more room than is provided to list your work experience, attach an additional sheet of paper. Be sure that you use the same format utilized in the application; that you clearly mark which item you are supplementing; and that your name is on the attached sheet of paper. Make a note at the bottom of the application that there are attachments, just in case the papers become separated.

Physical data. Always answer in the units (feet, inches, pounds, etc.) requested on the application. If units are not specified, indicate what units you are using. Be careful when you answer questions about medical problems. If a problem was serious, it might be wise to attach a statement from the attending physician that the condition was cleared up, will present no further problems, etc.

To determine whether or not you have a problem, be aware of the company's physical requirements. Talking about the problem face-to-face with the interviewer would be to your advantage. It is important that you be able to show that you have controlled your condition and that it will not interfere with your job performance. Bring a written report from your doctor (preferably a specialist) to the interview.

Education and military service. These sections of the application do not call for complex or carefully weighed answers. Put down what you have done or are doing with regard to either school or military service (or both), if these are applicable. If you have done nothing concerning either of these areas, write "Not applicable."

Reason for wanting to work for this company. Think about this one before you answer it. Why do you? Why is the company in business? What can you do to help it attain its goals? Whatever your answer, do not make it extremely self-centered. Ask yourself what you would want to see in this space if you were an employer.

Ever applied here before? Answer truthfully. The question is not intended to screen you out; its purpose is to keep the records straight. Otherwise, the company may believe it has two or three applicants with the same name and thus may create files for each.

Prior conviction of a felony/misdemeanor. Being convicted of a felony is hard to hide. Avoid a lengthy explanation until your interview day, if you obtain one. Use only the facts in describing the incident. Do not interject any personal bias. And a good common-sense point: Find out if you have any violations on record anywhere before you decide to list any.

Nepotism. Some companies have a strict rule prohibiting relatives from working within the same company. If you are not sure whether or not this rule applies to you, call the company and ask.

Minimum salary. Most companies pay flight attendants according to a contractual rate. Simply state, "Current contract."

Desired location. In Chapter 4 you saw a partial list of flight attendant bases for specific companies. FAPA publishes a more complete list in its *Flight Attendant Directory of Employers.* Your natural impulse will be to determine where the airline bases its flight attendants, and that is fine, but do not indicate that you do not wish to be relocated. By telling an airline that you will not relocate, you are eliminating yourself from the hiring process. A fact of life in flight attending is that you can expect to be relocated at some time in your career.

Special interests and hobbies. Your avocational interests tell a lot about you as a person. Use this section to note any volunteer work experience and any special achievements or awards. Avoid mentioning any involvement with political, religious or controversial groups.

Photographs. If a photograph is required, a good snapshot or instant print will do. Dress for the picture as if going to an interview. When shooting a full-length picture, stand at the angle that is most flattering to you. Posture is important. Keep your head high and your shoulders straight. Submit a photograph only if required to do so. If you belong to a minority group (male, black, Hispanic, etc.), sending a picture with all applications and resumes may be to your advantage.

Essay questions. These questions require time and thought. Do not be concerned about right or wrong answers, as most companies are looking for content, spelling, penmanship, grammar and punctuation. In short, they want to know how well you express yourself verbally. Initially, write down your thoughts, regardless of how unorganized they may be. This exercise will help you construct a good answer later on. Ask friends and family for advice. Allow yourself a realistic amount of time to complete the questions.

General information. This section is the part of the application that will ask you if you have any friends or relatives working for the company. Having relatives working for the company may or may not be advantageous, depending on how closely related they are, what position they hold, how the company views their performance, and whether the company has an anti-nepotism policy.

Friends working for the company also may or may not benefit you. If their work record is good, the fact that they are friends will probably help.

Additional information. You may want to practice typing this information on another copy before you type the original application — just to see if everything fits in the allotted space.

Whether you type or print, be sure everything is legible. Do not use pencil or a script typewriter. Make sure that you have not overlooked any section that requires an answer in your own handwriting. You also may want someone else to proofread the application before you mail it to be certain there are no errors. Photocopy the final draft before you mail it, and keep the copy for your records.

On to the Interview: A Continuing Saga

The application process has just barely begun when you mail off your first applications. Some considerable amount of time could pass before you win an interview. Meantime, keep updating your application whenever doing so is appropriate. Most airlines keep applications on active status for a period ranging from six months to a year, so regular updating is necessary simply to make sure that you always have an active application on file. Other reasons for updating include:

- If you move.

- If you change telephone numbers.

- If you acquire additional education or add to your other qualifications.

While the process is going on, there is one thing above all that you will have to do: maintain your positive state of mind.

You need to have inner confidence in order to pursue a flight attending job relentlessly and do well during interviews. You might possibly be able to go through the motions of mailing off applications and resumes without being buoyed by the certainty, in your own mind, that your hard work will pay off. What you cannot do without real confidence is fool your interviewers; a tentative attitude will be apparent to airline personnel.

When hiring, airlines receive thousands of applications per week for the flight attendant position. Statistics show that one of every 80 people who submit applications is offered employment. With competition so intense, you owe it to yourself to be prepared, relaxed, and positive when you are called for an interview. Doing so will enable you to sell your most valuable asset: you.

There is no reason to be frightened. You are there to explore the possibilities; no one is there to embarrass you or to make you feel uncomfortable. The people interviewing you want you to feel comfortable and relaxed. They realize that they will not have the opportunity to know the "real you" if you are ill at ease and quite evidently nervous.

If you are scheduled for an airline interview, you should feel confident. After all, had your resume and application not met the company's qualifications and criteria, you would not have been scheduled. The airline obviously feels that you meet its broad qualifications. By getting the interview you have earned the right to feel confident and this confidence should show through.

There is a difference, however, between feeling confident and being aggressive and overbearing. The inner confidence that is formed through anticipation and preparation will help you to relax and to feel good about the interview situation.

There are three sides to your preparation: emotional (psychological); mental (intellectual) and physical (your "look"). Taking care of No. 3 can do wonders in bolstering No.1. Airlines have an image that they want to foster and to protect; they achieve their goals in part through the image projected by their flight attendants, who are their most visible representatives most of the time for most of the travelling public. The flight attendant image includes a number of elements but it begins with the right look.

Your appearance can convey confidence, organization, status, authority productivity, and control of a situation. It can convey "the company image."

That is our next topic: appearance.

CHAPTER 7

Fine-Tuning Your Image

Once your application and resume have been processed and you are among the competitive candidates for a position, you will be scheduled for the interview process. Preparing yourself for the initial meeting may be one of the most important steps you will take toward landing your new job.

First impressions are lasting; that concept still holds true. There is an old saying in personnel that hiring decisions are often made in the first 30 seconds of the interview, and the balance of the time is used to justify that decision. Since first impressions almost always are based on a reaction to your appearance, the employer should sense a total effect of which you are in control: a well-groomed, well-prepared, well-presented professional image.

In some jobs, qualifications are all that count. However, according to an article in *The New York Times* entitled "Dressing to Get a Job," neatness was the No. 1 recommendation of people who handle hiring. A woman executive was quoted as saying, "If their appearance isn't neat, their qualifications aren't good enough." This rule applies to most jobs, but it is rigidly applied in public contact jobs. The flight attendant position is 100 percent public contact. Therefore, common sense indicates that appearance is a vital part of being competitive for the position. Your first overall visual impact will determine the tone of the interview or evaluation process.

A few nuggets to chew on:

- If you want the interviewer to believe that you matter, you must dress as though you do matter.

- Your clothes and the way you wear them should provide a winning backdrop for the product you are selling: YOURSELF.

- The "statement" made by your clothes and bearing may not tell as much about you as your qualifications do, but it nonetheless will be the most powerful initial message. If it is negative, you may not be able to overcome it.

- When you look good, you feel good and generally are at your best.

- A good appearance is a healthy appearance: Your hair, skin, nails, complexion and teeth all reflect the state of your health and vitality.

- The professional image of any person seeking an airline career should be dealt with in all aspects, including:
  - Effective wardrobe planning
  - Cosmetic application
  - Good grooming in relation to hair style
  - Accessorizing
  - Body language
  - Motivation

Physical criteria

Before you can be certain of making a great first impression, you have to know that you meet basic physical criteria of the airline company.

Unlike many other businesses, airlines have very specific physical criteria to which they adhere when selecting future employees. If you do not meet these criteria, you generally will not be considered for the next step of the hiring process.

All but one of the physical categories that are "graded" by interviewers fall under the heading of image. The one exception is eyesight, and even this is not really an exception. One aspect of poor eyesight is that the seeing-impaired individual cannot seem efficient in most of the activities undertaken by flight attendants. If you will call to mind the original purpose of flight attendants, the image problem created by seriously impaired eyesight will be self-evident; passengers cannot be reassured by a person rendered inefficient by poor eyesight.

The basic physical qualifications of an airline either are outlined in the pre-employment material that comes with the application or are printed on the application itself. If you are uncertain about the meaning of some of the information, do not hesitate to call the employment office and ask for clarification of the guidelines. You need to be absolutely sure that you meet the requirements instead of wasting your valuable time and that of the interviewer on a fruitless meeting.

Height & weight. Flight attendant candidates usually are weighed and measured at each interview session and at the airline physical — wearing clothing. In most cases, you will be allowed to remove a suit jacket and your shoes.

If you have a weight problem, do not interview until you have shed the excess weight. (If you have an excuse for being over the maximum weight for your height, such as a recent pregnancy, the airline will listen to it as a reason for postponing an interview, but they will expect you to meet height-weight restrictions when you do show up.)

If you are concerned about being too thin, relax; the airlines can fit any size that is within their hiring guidelines.

Both men and women who have lifted weights or performed other exercise to the point of adding muscle weight could have a problem with weight requirements, which are adhered to strictly for both sexes.

Meeting weight guidelines continues to be a requirement throughout a flight attendant's career. Airlines prefer not to hire applicants with potential weight problems since these problems could persist and pose an ever-present threat of losing a flight attendant.

Complexion. Your complexion should be clear, with no blemishes or noticeable scars. Because of their use of makeup, women have the advantage in meeting this criterion.

If you have a distracting, persistent acne problem, you should consult a dermatologist to have the condition remedied before you interview for a job. For severe acne scarring, there are procedures (through a physician) to "sand" and smooth the skin. Beware: This course of action can cause you as much as three weeks of real pain. You have to want a clear complexion very badly to submit yourself to this cure.

There should be no distracting or disfiguring scars on the face, the hands, the arms or, for women, the legs.

Your teeth. Teeth are expected to be white, clean and relatively even to present a nice smile. If your teeth have grayed through the use of medication, check with your dentist to see how you may be able to remedy the condition. If your teeth are extremely crooked, your dentist or orthodontist may recommend braces. Make sure that braces or retainers are off your teeth before you interview. Most airlines will not hire a person who is wearing braces. (Since there are exceptions, you might try checking with the employment office prior to your interview.)

Vision. Both corrected and uncorrected vision must meet the particular carrier's requirements. This information cannot be falsified. A vision exam is part of the pre-employment physical. Generally, glasses will be allowed on the job if the frames have been approved by management. Contacts are also acceptable. Consult your eye doctor about contacts that are more wearable for the flying environment. Contacts can be tinted if the color is a natural one.

If you have determined that you meet the physical criteria for the job you want, you now are ready to begin your wardrobe and image planning.

Effective Wardrobe Planning/Women

When in doubt about what to wear to your interview, always revert to common sense, remembering that your goal is to present a professional, businesslike appearance. Airline uniforms are conservative and "classic" in style. The clothing you select to wear should emulate the simple, clean lines of the uniform styles that you see being worn by flight attendants.

Several factors should be weighed as you make a final selection on what garment to wear:

* How does the color look on you?

* Is the line of the garment congruent with your body shape?

* Do you have proper accessories to go with the outfit?

Color. Have you had one of those days when you felt great but people kept asking you if you were a bit under the weather? Or conversely, have you had a day when you did not feel well at all, yet people kept complimenting you on how terrific you looked? The colors you were wearing may have been responsible.

If you have had a color analysis done, use your color chart when choosing the basic color for the appropriate interview attire. If you have not had a color analysis done, you may want to consider submitting to the process. The analysis will be your first step in educating yourself in how to build a wardrobe based on a color scheme. This method of wardrobe building will save you money by permitting you to select fewer, but higher-quality, pieces of clothing that all coordinate. Be sure to consult with a reputable person when having the analysis done.

You should choose colors in your palette that are subtle and have authority, such as gray, navy blue, charcoal, beige or tweed. It is best to be conservative in your color selection. Remember, the darker the color, the more authority it transmits. Stay away from black, as this choice will be overpowering.

When choosing a fabric, select one that will travel well and will endure many hours of sitting without looking "slept in." Consider the time of year and choose either a light or a heavy fabric to coincide with the season. (You know this already, but a heavy fabric in hot weather will leave you very much the worse for wear by the time you make it into the room with your interviewer. There is no point in creating a liability for yourself.)

Stay away from loud colors and large prints; also, avoid soft pastels, as these tones may convey an impression of weakness or indecisiveness.

Body shape. After determining a color scheme, take a good look at your body shape. If you believe it is perfect, then perhaps you can put anything on and have it look great. Since most of us lack that perfect shape, we have to "create" a perfect look. We create illusions to disguise what we perceive to be imperfections, such as narrow shoulders, wide hips, heavy thighs, or being too tall or too short.

For example, balance between the upper and lower body is attainable through illusions. For narrow shoulders, add shoulder pads; for a long waist, wear a belt that is the same color as your skirt; for a short waist, elongate it by wearing a belt the same color as the blouse. You have not changed your body, but you have changed the impression made by your figure simply through wise selection of clothes and accessories.

Through our clothes, we can hide the things we do not like and accentuate those traits that we do like. With the right clothes, you can appear taller, heavier, thinner, or whatever your particular need may be.

BODY SHAPES

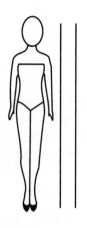   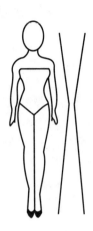 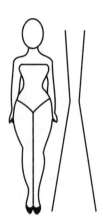

Slim build   Stockier build   Full figure build   Full figure with wider hips build

Suits. According to John T. Mulloy's book *Dress for Success*, the business uniform for women is the skirted suit. As a rule, you should be conservative in your selection. The business suit will establish authority, credibility and likeability. As noted, the darker the color, the more authority it communicates.

If possible, make an investment in a good basic suit in your color scheme and in a classic style. Shop carefully for a garment that is well made and fits as if it were designed for you (even though it may require some alterations by the store's tailor). A baggy or oversized outfit looks unkempt. A suit that is too snug could send off one of two messages: that your weight is on the rise or that you usually wear your clothes too tight.

Keep in mind also that hemlines can be trendy. Avoid the trendy and choose a safe length, right below the knee. If you are in doubt about a garment because it seems trendy or unusual, do not buy it. You are trying to make the right verbal statement. Trendy clothing says something about your personality that may be regarded by an interviewer as unprofessional or frivolous. Unusual clothing draws attention to itself, not to the individual wearing it. Too casual a fashion may project the notion that you are casual about work.

Remember that a single-breasted jacket is more slimming. A double-breasted jacket will give the illusion of a heavier appearance. Make these illusions work for you to "slim" or "add weight" as appropriate.

Depending on the cut of the suit, the suit jacket should fall below your buttocks, especially if you are trying to de-emphasize this area.

Ensure that your suit is pressed and wrinkle-free, with all factory threads and tags trimmed. Carry a lint remover with you to ensure a picture-perfect appearance.

The key in deciding what fashion is appropriate and how it should be worn is to remember that the people interviewing you are trying to visualize how you will represent the company. Make that visualization as easy as possible; give the professional, businesslike impression which they look for when hiring flight attendants.

Blouses. While selecting a suit, keep on the lookout for several coordinating blouses within the range of your color palette to complement what you achieve through suit selection. Two or three coordinating blouses in a conservative style (not too low or frilly) will afford you the flexibility of being prepared for several interviews over a two- to three-day period. A good basic suit can take on different looks with different skirts, blouses and accessories. Another consideration: While wearing the same suit to multiple interviews on consecutive days at an airline is perfectly acceptable, wearing the same blouse could be interpreted as a tell-tale sign of poor personal hygiene.

Dresses. If you choose to wear a dress, it should be worn with a coordinating jacket.

Patterns add interest to clothing, but subtle patterns are more suitable for business. Large or colored prints should be avoided. If you pair a dress or blouse with a patterned jacket, the patterns should coordinate. Be very careful when combining patterns.

Choose fabrics that are businesslike. Either sheer or clingy fabrics will be inappropriate. Garments that are too tight or too revealing are not appropriate for business, either.

The neckline should not be too low-cut.

Jackets. When you are purchasing a suit jacket or a jacket to coordinate with other garments, watch for the following attributes to be sure that the jacket flatters you from every angle.

- Make sure the jacket flatters your skin and your blouse color. If you stay within your color palette, you will not have to be concerned, with one caveat: Jackets should be in the basic and neutral colors of your palette.

- Unless your pattern is matched at the seams, it will have an out-of-balance, cheap look. Again, the pattern should be conservative.

82   Flight Attendant

Blouses

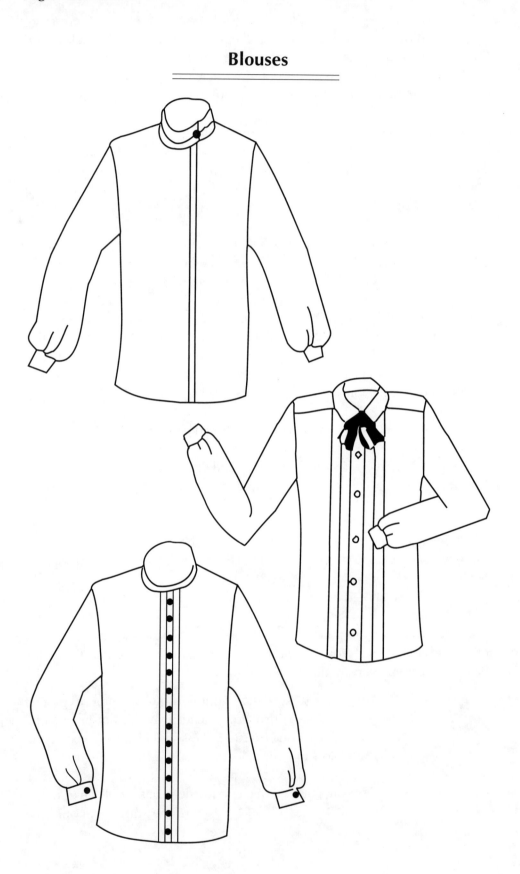

- Women's jackets come in a number of cuts and styles. Be sure to choose cut and style that flatter your body shape. In creating the illusion that you want others to see, you probably should make certain that the bottom edge of the jacket falls below the widest part of your lower torso so that you can look as slim as possible. If you struggle with wide hips, as 75 percent of American women do, a jacket that is either shorter or longer than the point where your hips flare will create a good look.

- Update your lapel width. If you are wearing an older, slightly dated suit, it should be one with classic lines and the quality to last; in the alternative, where appropriate, you might pay a seamstress or tailor to narrow wide lapels to update yesterday's style.

- Check to be sure that the edge of your sleeve just covers your wrist bone.

- A wool or wool blend looks best and is the most durable fabric.

Skirts. Like jackets, skirts should be in the basic and neutral colors of your palette to make them more versatile. Choose a color that flatters your blouse and jacket colors.

Patterned skirts should be kept conservative for business. Patterns should be on the right scale for your body. For instance, if you are a small person, wear small prints. If you are larger, your patterns can be larger, too.
Skirts that fall below the knees will be most suitable for a business meeting (your interview is such a meeting).

Handbags. The handbag you choose is an important part of your total image. You may be perfectly dressed, yet if you are carrying the wrong handbag or briefcase, your outfit can look second-rate or poorly coordinated. Again, stay within your palette and the specific color scheme you have chosen for your business clothing.

Choose a leather handbag in a basic color, such as black, tan, taupe or cordovan.

Your bag or briefcase should be in proportion to your own size. It has been said that the more petite the woman, the larger the handbag that she tends to choose. This incongruity may be fine for some situations, but not for a place of business. On a scale proportioned to your height and frame, the most appropriate handbag is a small to medium-sized, satchel-type bag with handles and a shoulder strap.

Jackets

Skirts

Many women prefer to carry a briefcase and a purse, but this overload should be avoided, if possible, so that you will be able to shake hands without appearing to do a juggling act to get one hand free.

If you carry a briefcase, choose a basic color, such as black, camel or cordovan. A wallet, brush and lipstick can be slipped inside your briefcase for storage and easy accessibility.

A messy purse or briefcase reflects on the person carrying it, so take a few minutes to organize the contents in preparation for the interview.

Shoes. Footwear should be coordinated with your suit but does not necessarily have to be the same color. Black, taupe and cordovan are safe, conservative colors. Avoid coordinating reds, blues, greens, etc., to your outfit. This will not appear businesslike.

The proper shoe will pull your whole image together. A pump-type shoe is the most appropriate style. A pump with an open toe or sling-back style also would be considered acceptable. The shoe should be in a classic style with little ornamentation. Do not wear clogs, wedges, sandals or dyed-to-match fabric shoes. And you might as well go barefoot as to wear a cocktail shoe.

Your shoes should have a fresh shine and be mounted on soles and heels that are in good repair.

Accessories. Your accessories are important because they can either accent or subvert your professional image. Trendy accessories are appropriate to accent trendy clothing and should not be coordinated with business attire. The fewer your accessories, the more credible you will be. Excessive adornment bespeaks an insecurity in you. Choose simple accessories that bring out the best in the clothing you are wearing and that make a positive statement about you as a potential flight attendant for this employer.

Many women make the mistake of not accessorizing. The money spent on accessories is as important as the investment in your clothing. Accessories pull an outfit together and add polish.

When choosing accessories, you should have one center of interest to which your other accessories are subordinate.

- *Jewelry.* Airlines have regulations about how much and what kinds of jewelry their flight attendants can wear. Even at your interview, your jewelry should be consonant with the airline image. Gold and pearls are the most appropriate types of jewelry to wear, but keep pieces small and simple. One earring per ear is a safe guideline to follow, and wear only one ring per hand. Use common sense. Bangle or charm bracelets that make noise can be distracting and draw too much attention during an interview.

One other thing: Bracelets and rings will draw attention to your hands and fingernails. Make sure they deserve all this attention.

- *Belts.* Belts add polish to your outfit. As mentioned earlier, they also can help to create illusions about body shape.

  Summarizing:

  - If you have a thick waist, look for garments that have matching belts; avoid skinny or fussy belts.
  - If you are short-waisted, match the color of your belt to your blouse to create the illusion of a longer torso.
  - If you are long-waisted, match the color of your belt to your skirt to give the illusion of a shorter torso.
  - If you have a small waist, you can accentuate it by wearing belts in contrasting colors.

- *Scarves.* Scarves are wonderful accessories. You can change your whole look by changing scarves or by adding one.

  Since scarves can be tied in hundreds of different ways, the same scarf can give you many different looks. Illustrated on the next page are conservative styles and tying instructions suitable for business attire. You have considerable latitude within the airline industry's fundamentally conservative approach to wearing scarves. But do not be too flamboyant in your selection of patterns or tying style. The scarf should flatter your outfit and face, not overpower you.

  When selecting a scarf, bear in mind that silk scarves will last the longest and are the easiest with which to work. Choose a high-quality scarf that will coordinate with several outfits.

Undergarments. Wear proper undergarments, such as a bra, slip, panties and anything else appropriate. Undergarments, even though not seen, are a must. There is always a chance of having a physical on the same day as your interview. Save yourself the embarrassment of not being appropriately prepared.

Hosiery. Hosiery is a part of a professional image. Not wearing it, no matter how great your tan may be or how terrible the weather is, would be totally out of step. Wear skin-toned nylons, not colored or trendy ones. Nylons with reinforced toes in an open-toe shoe are as distracting as slips that show beneath skirts and bra straps that have slipped off shoulders.

Ties and Scarves

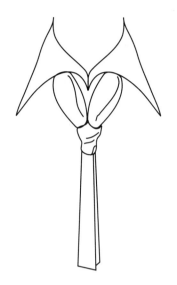

Necktie

1. Place the tie around your neck with one end longer than the other. (Let the wide end of the tie hang lower if it is a tapered tie.)

2. Cross the longer end over and under the shorter end.

3. Then cross the long end back over the short end.

4. Slip the long end up and through the "V" at the neck.

5. Push the end through the knot from above and tighten the knot.

6. Adjust tie to fit the collar or wear it low with an open collar.

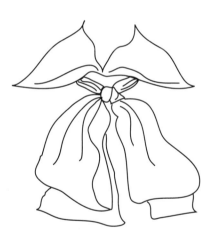

Artist Bow

Place the scarf under the collar. Bring ends to front and simply tie a big fluffy bow. The ends should not extend much beyond bow.

Ascot Bow

Tie an oblong scarf as in the necktie but omit step 5.

Effective Wardrobe Planning/Men

Projecting a confident and professional image should be a high priority for a man when he is preparing for a flight attendant interview.

Men's fashion in the business world has little flexibility; the rules are simple but must be followed punctiliously.

According to Mulloy's *Dress for Success*, the proper business attire is the two-piece suit. Colors to choose from are very standard: gray, navy blue, charcoal or tweed. Choose natural fibers, such as linen, gabardine, tweed or wool, and make sure you buy high-quality, well-made garments, which will look better and last longer than poorer stuff.

Make sure that the jacket covers your buttocks and that the inside lining does not hang below the jacket. The shoulder seam should extend $1/4$ to $1/2$ inch over the natural shoulder line. Be certain, too, that there is ample room in the shoulders, back and sleeves. The garment should not be too tight nor too baggy; it should fit. Clothes that do not fit do not yield a professional appearance.

The sleeve should end at the top of your wrist. Avoid plastic buttons. Snip all tags and loose threads and have your jacket steam-cleaned for the best results. The pants should have a slight break in front. Check the seat; if it is baggy, have the pants altered before wearing them. Pockets should be smooth-fitting, with no flopping or bowing.

Pants should be well-pressed, and pleats should be smooth.

Shirts. Solids and pinstripes are the safest and most widely accepted looks. White or light blue are the best colors to wear. For the right fit, make sure that you can insert one finger between the collar and your neck. If you have a long neck, you can wear a high collar. Short collars work better for short necks and faces. Cuffs should show a quarter-inch below the sleeve of your jacket. If you are wearing cuff links, avoid "gawky" ones. Do not wear short sleeves with a jacket or coat. Make sure your shirts are neatly pressed.

Ties. A tie should enhance your suit, pull your look together, and add a touch of color. Do not skimp on this item. Buy the best you can afford in a natural fabric. A $3 1/2$ inch tie is standard for interviews. Bow ties are out of place. Choose a tie with a small pattern — dots, stripes, paisley or foulard — to add interest to your suit. When tied, your tie should end at the middle or bottom of your belt.

Belts. A good-looking leather belt of high quality is a must for every suit. Buy the best you can afford in a style that is one to $1 1/2$ inches wide with a discreet

Ties

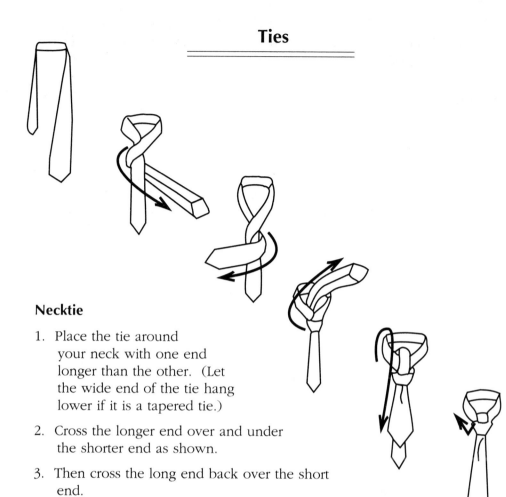

Necktie

1. Place the tie around your neck with one end longer than the other. (Let the wide end of the tie hang lower if it is a tapered tie.)

2. Cross the longer end over and under the shorter end as shown.

3. Then cross the long end back over the short end.

4. Slip the long end up and through the "V" at the neck.

5. Push the end through the knot from above and tighten the knot.

6. Adjust tie to fit the collar.

gold or silver buckle. The color should be black or brown. A belt color matching that of your shoes is the most accepted way of making a selection. The belt buckle should be "classic" and simple.

Pocket scarves. The pocket scarf sets off your tie. It should never be identical in pattern to the tie.

Jewelry. A man's watch should be gold or silver and of good quality. Leave those plastic sport watches with alarms at home. Rings should not be chunky or flashy. Constrain yourself to a wedding band, a class ring, or a signet ring. You do not want to come into your interview sparkling. The less jewelry, the better.

Wallets. Be sure that your wallet is reasonably flat and in good condition. A quality leather wallet looks good with everything from suits to jeans.

Briefcases. Leather is best, hard or soft. No aluminum, no plastics. A briefcase carries a message about you. Bring the best or bring none at all.

Socks. These should be matched to either your shoes or your pants. They should be inconspicuous and coordinate in texture and color with your suit. They should extend over the calf to ensure that no skin shows when you sit down or cross your legs.

Shoes. A nice loafer or a wing-tip is an appropriate style — a neutral color, well polished, well kept. Check the heels for good repair.

When wardrobe has been established, you are not yet "home free." For men and women alike, an important consideration in physical image is the hair. For women, another factor — and a very important one — is makeup.

Makeup: A Mandatory Art

As an enhancement to a woman's natural beauty, makeup is part of a polished professional image. It also serves as protection from such conditions as wind, sun, a cold climate, and the dry environment of an aircraft cabin.

The wearing of makeup is required while a flight attendant is in uniform. It lends credibility to the professionalism conveyed by the uniform.

Most airlines require that:

- Your makeup be tasteful and compatible with your skin coloring, your hair, and the uniform.

- Your makeup be fresh and carefully applied to create a businesslike appearance.

- An overly-made-up look be avoided.

The minimum cosmetics for a professional, polished appearance are a foundation or base makeup; a blusher or rouge; lipstick; and eye makeup, to include one or more of the following: shadow, eyeliner, mascara or natural-looking false eyelashes.

You must decide how to apply your makeup and how much of it to wear to your interview. If you do not now wear makeup, consult a professional and learn how to apply it in a way that flatters your facial structure and skin tone. Too many people make the mistake of wearing either no makeup or very little of it, then telling the recruiter that they are "willing to learn." Wanting to learn is admirable, but makeup is a way of life in the airline world.

Makeup professionals come in many price ranges, so choose one to suit your budget. Cosmetics firms train representatives to apply makeup at counters in department stores. This service is performed at no charge to the customer except for the items the customer chooses to buy, and these consultations can be helpful. There are, of course, independent consultants who specialize in makeup application, but be prepared to pay a premium for their services.

Use daytime makeup techniques that look natural and businesslike. Eye shadow should be neutral. Do not use bright colors even if you feel they are fashionable or toney. It is not uncommon to remember people by their most outstanding characteristics. No one wants to be remembered mainly for her eye shadow — and certainly not when her objective is a job in flight attending.

Recruiters are well aware that makeup instruction is part of the flight training course. Their fear, however, can be that you perhaps prefer not to wear makeup or, worse still, that you like the way you look using too much of it. Both extremes of taste are hard to change.

Face Shapes

Square

Rectangular

Oval

Heart

Triangular

Round

Your Face Shape/Women

There are six basic face shapes. Identifying your face shape will help you determine the most flattering earring style, hair style, eyeglass frame, and neckline shape for you.

Defining your face shape can be difficult because it is not uncommon for a person to have more than one shape in combination rather than a single "true" face shape. In this situation, follow the guidelines for the prevailing shape. A friend may be able to help you identify what this shape is; or you can use a mirror, pulling your hair away from your face and looking at the angles and curves. As you look in the mirror, cover the lower third of your face. Then, for a final determination, uncover the the lower part.

Fashion designers and airline hiring departments consider the oval face to be the best possible type. Your objective, if you do not have an oval face, is to create an "oval illusion" through hair style, choice of accessories, and neck line.

Following are some tips on how to manage various face shapes.

Square face. A square face is as wide at the forehead as it is at the jaw, and it is as wide as it is long. Your task is to create an illusion of length and to soften the impact of your jaw and your forehead.

Hair: A soft style with fullness on top will add height and will sleek out the jaw line to minimize width.

Earrings: Soft, rounded shapes are right; avoid squares. Dangle earrings will give you more length as well as a shape that is longer than it is wide.

Eyeglasses: Rounded shapes are best. Buy frames that extend out past the cheekbones.

Neck lines: Soften the angles of the face by wearing soft jewel or cowl necks.

Rectangular face. A rectangular face is the same width at the forehead, cheekbones and jaw line. The face is oblong, and your goal is to add width to your face, creating the illusion of less length.

Hair: Add fullness on the sides. Avoid piling your hair up or in other ways adding height to the top of your head.

Earrings: Choose soft, rounded shapes. Avoid dangles.

Eyeglasses: Reduce the length of your face by choosing frames that are wide and heavy, with soft angles.

Neck lines: Avoid V-neck or open collars; choose soft neck lines.

Oval face. An oval face is considered the perfect face shape. It is wider at the forehead than at the chin and tapers from the cheekbones to the chin.

Hair: Use long or short cuts, angled at the jaw line to accentuate the cheek bones. An oval face can accommodate a style that adds width.

Earrings: Choose curves and angles; avoid anything long and dangling that may throw your face shape out of balance.

Eyeglasses: The frame should be no wider than the widest part of the face.

Neck lines: Any neck line that is not too severe is right for you.

Heart face. This face has a wide forehead, high cheek lines, and a narrow chin. There is usually a widow's peak at the forehead.

Hair: Choose a style that is loose and full and that falls below the chin. Hide the width of the forehead with soft bangs and keep a part off to one side.

Earrings: Oval or rounded will work best. Triangular or teardrop earrings are also good because they will add width to the jaw line.

Eyeglasses: Select oval or rounded shapes. The width of the frame should be greater at the bottom.

Neck lines: Add width to your lower face with boat or bateau neck lines.

Triangular face. This type of face is wider at the chin and jaw line than at the forehead.

Hair: Add width to the forehead by choosing a style that is full on top and on the sides; such hairstyles will balance your face.

Earrings: Choose a shape that is wider at the top. Your earrings should be angular, e.g., long and narrow or even rectangular.

Eyeglasses: Add width with wide frames to give balance to the face.

Neck lines: Choose V-necks and open collars.

Round face. This is a very full face, one that is as long as it is wide. The goal is to create an illusion of length and slim the face.

Hair: Add height on top and keep fullness above the ears. Long and layered or short styles that add height are best.

Earrings: Any angles that can be added to the face will break down the "roundness." Wear angular earrings, e.g., long, narrow shapes or rectangles.

Eyeglasses: Buy angular-shaped glasses.

Neck lines: Choose V-necks and open collars to lengthen your face.

Your Face Shape/Men

In the quest for an "oval illusion," men have only their hair to work with. Your hair is a frame that will either emphasize or enhance your facial characteristics. For men as for women, the easiest way to determine your face shape is to look at the upper two-thirds of your facial structure by pulling back your hair and observing the curves and angles. As you look in the mirror, hide the lower third of your face. For final objectivity, look at your entire face and finalize your decision.

The following hints will help with your hair styling.

Rectangular: You need a cut that adds width to your face. This effect can be achieved by a rounder cut, leaving the hair longer and fuller on the sides and longer in the back.

Round: Your cut should narrow your face. A good method for doing this is to brush back the hair from your forehead, with a partial part or no part. Sideburns should be short.

Heart: This face shape has a broad forehead and narrow jaw. The face can be balanced by eliminating a lot of hair on top. Clip the hair in layers on the top and the sides.

Triangular: An inverted version of the heart-shaped face, the triangular face can be balanced by wearing the hair longer and fuller on the top and the sides.

Square face: This type of face can look good in almost any cut, as it usually has great eyes, jaw lines and cheekbones. Decide which feature you like best and emphasize it through the cut of your hair.

Oval face: If you have this face, you can wear just about any hair style that is comfortable.

The following general remarks about men's hair styles encompass a point of view that should not be forgotten as you get yourself ready for your interview. The reason: The point of view at issue is that of the airline world.

To project a professional image, hair, without exception, should be cut and styled to bring out the accents of your face. It should be short and conservative and cut so as to fall properly in place, and it must not fall into the eyes. As a matter of course, it should be neat and clean.

When you are having your hair styled, there are some guidelines to follow if you want to be in step with airline hair regulations:

- The back should not extend any farther down than the top of the collar; it may cover the upper half of the ear provided that the hair falls close to your head.

- If you keep your hair at the extreme length allowed in back, it should be neatly blocked or tapered.

- Sideburns should not extend below the bottom of the earlobe; they should be light to moderate in thickness and should not be extreme in style.

- "Mutton chops" are not acceptable.

- Afro hairstyles should not extend more than two inches from the scalp.

Finally, the following hints may help you in handling hair texture.

- Thick, straight hair should be properly trimmed to avoid a wild "scarecrow" look.

- Thick, curly hair should be cut shorter to maintain a well-groomed appearance.

- If your hair is thinning, it should be cut short. A short cut will make it look fuller. Keep your sideburns short.

- For fine hair, a short cut will be much more controllable.

There is another area of hair for men to consider: facial hair. Airlines have strict guidelines regulating facial hair.

A moustache is acceptable if kept neatly trimmed. It should not extend below the corners of the mouth or over the top of the lip line. Handlebar or Fu Man Chu styles are not acceptable. Neither are beards and goatees.

Your face must appear clean and well-shaven. This requirement creates something of a dilemma for men who have a beard and are hesitant about shaving it off for an interview. Only you can determine how deeply you want the position. If you want the job, you have to be willing to project the total image.

For Women and Men

Paying attention to every detail of your overall grooming is of cardinal importance. Several details that apply to both women and men cannot be overlooked if you expect to give your best impression in an interview.

Hands and nails. Hands and nails should be meticulously cared for and nails well trimmed. Nails should be neither too long nor too short. They should be polished and/or manicured. Nail biters should overcome the habit prior to an interview since bitten nails detract from a professional appearance. Designs on your fingernails, chipped nails, or nails polished with extreme colors are not acceptable.

Remember: Rings will attract attention to the hands and nails. If your hands and nails are exquisitely kept, the attention will be to your advantage. If they are substandard, it will not.

Personal hygiene. Interviewing is a nerve-wracking, stressful situation. Ensure that you have a good deodorant or antiperspirant so you do not show how nervous you really are.

If you have halitosis, bring mints or breath spray to freshen with at opportune moments, being sure to be discreet. Do not chew gum.

Make sure that your clothes are pressed and properly cleaned. Hotels will provide irons and ironing boards for pressing out unwanted wrinkles if you are staying overnight prior to your interview. If your clothes have been in cedar or mothball storage, air them outside, if weather permits, until the odor has vanished. If your clothes are dirty, by all means have them cleaned. Do not take any chances on any omission that could detract from the band box image you are trying to project.

For women: Legs and underarms should be free of hair. Not only is this good personal hygiene; it is mandatory for the flight attendant position.

Hosiery/socks. Nylons and socks are part of a professional appearance and self-presentation. You will be weighed at some point, a procedure requiring that you remove your shoes. Women: Be sure that your nylons have no runs or snags (always bring along an extra pair). Men: Socks should match one another and not be threadbare at the heels or toes.

Fragrance. Perfume, cologne, after-shave lotion — these items should be used conservatively. Use light scents that are not too strong or exotic.

Eyeglasses. As noted, glasses are permitted by most airlines. Some require contact lenses, but glasses are permitted with a recommendation from a personal physician if you are unable to wear contact lenses in flight. Generally, all eyeglass frames must be approved by a member of in-flight management. Frames must be plain, with a contemporary style, preferably in gold or tortoiseshell. Extreme styles are not acceptable. Darkly shaded lenses also are not acceptable, although some tints may be approved.

These details of airline rules for flight attendants are good for you to know prior to an interview. Knowledge of them will help you choose the right kind of glasses. Obviously, you should leave trendy or unusual eyeglasses at home.

And as a matter of common sense: Do not interview wearing sunglasses. One man sat for two hours in a dimly lighted interview room wearing polarized glasses. Although he may have believed he was very "cool," the recruiter did not share such an opinion.

CHAPTER 8

Preparing Yourself Mentally

As important as they are, your "looks" are only one part of the image you create. From the first moment when you meet with an interviewer, you are communicating in three different ways: through content (what you say), through attitude (how you say it), and through body language (how you react to the stress of having to say it to this person under these circumstances). All three of these modes of communicating can be strengthened by preparing yourself.

Getting Psyched, Getting Smart

Two of the keys to a successful interview, and part of the image you will present, are the psychological and intellectual aspects of your presentation. Beyond the confidence-building you have done by developing your physical image, you can build your confidence for the interview in two other basic ways:

by "psyching yourself up" for the interview and by anticipating the kinds of questions that will be asked.

Psyching yourself up can help you appear calm, cool and collected. This activity works best, however, if it is combined with a sort of "psyching down."

Each time you interview, you should approach the interview as if this opportunity represents "the job" you desire and "the company" for which you want to work. At the same time, in counterbalance to this frame of mind, you should stay conscious of the fact that not only is the airline looking you over, but you are doing the same thing with regard to the airline. Your plan is that, ultimately, you will select the airline that offers you the best possibilities.

You are attempting the ultimate "hard sell" and the ultimate "shopping spree" at the same time. You are trying to sell the airline on yourself as one of its flight attendants and on yourself as somebody who has chosen this airline and its company culture over all other airlines and their ways of life. You are trying to make this sale through your attitude and bearing rather than through flattery.

Simultaneously, to keep yourself calm, you are trying to get one part of your mind to remain a comparative shopper. "In the end, after all possibilities are explored," you are telling yourself, "the choice is mine. I decide where I am going to spend my career."

This balance of inner tensions will give you both a winning attitude and a saving presence of mind. It will stamp your image with conviction and confidence as well.

The other primary way to build your confidence is intellectually, by anticipating the types of information and questions you will encounter during the course of the interview. If you can anticipate accurately, you will be more likely to give a response that will create a positive impression.

One of the best preparations you can make, from an intellectual standpoint, is to learn a good bit about the company with which you are interviewing. Generally, information about the company, together with a job description, is sent to you along with the application form. Read this information! Local libraries may be able to complete your pre-interview education on this airline that is considering you as one of its flight attendants. If you feel that you need still more information, take a field trip to the airport and talk to some of the airline's employees. They will share the good and the bad with you and tell you exactly what you need to know about the job itself.

The knowledge that you gain in these ways will make you stand out from other applicants. Potential employers are always pleased when you know a good deal about the company — and are always displeased when you know nothing. Elementary psychology is at work here: Sales representatives who deal with corporate clientele are taught that before calling on a prospective new client, they should know almost as much about the company as its own senior executives do. While there are reasons for the salesperson's "cramming" for a sales call beyond those that govern your situation, most of the basic needs of the sales representative are your needs, too, and much of the same psychology applies. You will score "points" by knowing a lot about the company.

For yourself, too, the knowledge will pay off when you reach decision time. If you truly know the airlines that are competing for your services (assuming that you are lucky enough to have more than one job offer), your decision may be a very easy one.

Body Blows Can Be Telling

There is an old saying in the boxing business: "Kill the body and the head will die." What the saying means is that if enough hard blows are landed on an opponent's body, they will wear him down. At this point, one's attack can be turned against the opponent's head to score a knockout.

Something roughly analogous can happen to you if you give off the wrong body language during an interview, except that you will be doing it to yourself. No matter what your head tells your tongue to say, if your body is saying the opposite, you will suffer a knockout in your interview. And you will have struck the blows yourself through inappropriate body language.

Body language and spoken language are dependent on each other. No better single illustration can be given than that of a poker player who is bluffing. Verbally, the player "raises" the pot of money at stake as if he or she feels certain of having a winning hand. The player is trying to bluff other players at the table into folding (laying down their cards in defeat). If anything in the player's voice inflection or body language permits an opponent to see that the player is bluffing, the opponent will seize the upper hand; instead of folding, he or she will keep raising the stakes until the bluff collapses.

You can lose a lot of money by "giving away" your bluff. And you can lose your chance to land your dream job if your body language is not up to par.

The way to keep it up to par is to be aware of the messages given off by your habitual body language and to be aware also of what can happen to your body language under stress. Along with awareness, of course, you will need to practice the right body language, including the best ways of positioning yourself in the interview room in order to avoid the pitfalls of negative body vibes.

Make no mistake about this: You will be judged on poise and polish in your interview. You already know how to look polished. Do you know how to act polished? Can you keep your poise?

The answer to the latter question is "Yes, you can, if you are well prepared." Following are some hints for preparing yourself to give off the right body vibes.

- When you enter a room, you should obtain respectful, positive attention. You can achieve this attention through the way you present yourself. First off, you must have an upright, straightforward gait, with your eyes looking at the person meeting you. Appear relaxed, show an easy smile and happy appearance, and shake hands properly.

- The handshake is a story in itself. You should approach your interviewer with a confident smile and erect carriage, look directly into the interviewer's eyes, take his or her hand firmly, and shake hands as if you know you are somebody. Do not just place your hand in another person's hand and leave it there. Offer your hand in such a way that the interviewer knows you are interested in everything that is about to happen. As you take the interviewer's hand, address him or her with enthusiasm but not gushingly ["It's a pleasure to meet you, Mr./Ms./Mrs./Miss (Whoever)" or "Hi, I'm very happy to meet you, etc."]. Do these things and you will set the right tone for your interview.

- Do not sit down until invited to do so. Then sit erect, with your bottom all the way to the back of the chair. Lean slightly forward with your shoulders square and your arms and hands relaxed (not with arms crossed or hands clutching your purse or briefcase). Leaning forward shows an eagerness to listen, and the squared shoulders convey confidence. The open posture indicates confidence, an open attitude, and willingness to share and listen. By contrast, crossing your arms will create a visual impression of stubbornness and a closed mind, and holding onto some object can show insecurity and nervousness. Sit with your feet flat on the floor or crossed at the ankles. Such posture is professional and projects the right image. Not so the crossed, swinging leg, which betrays nervousness, indecision, insecurity, meekness, or a hyperactive, impatient disposition. And if you are female, the male interviewer may get the wrong message if too much leg is showing. Remember: You are a professional person seeking a career.

- In a group interview, show interest and enthusiasm by sitting near the front. You will be noticed more — and more positively.

People who gravitate to the back of the room are likely to be sized up as either non-participative or not good at mingling. Take active participation in all discussions, but do not be overbearing.

- Eye contact is of the utmost importance. It says you are in control and are definitely interested. Do not stare at the interviewer, however, because few people can bear to be gazed at directly for minutes on end. The time to look away from your interviewer's face briefly is during those moments when you are considering your answer to a question. Look to one side of the interviewer, and look up slightly, not down; then return your eyes to the face of your interviewer as you begin answering. Look at the entire person, not just into his or her eyes. Focus on various parts of the interviewer's face, thus establishing a rapport between the two of you.

- Verbally, you want to speak clearly, with good voice modulation. You also want to add constructively to the conversation, show an eagerness to perform, and project a genuine desire for the job.

For voice modulation, practice on a tape recorder. For avoidance of poor body language (flailing, sitting like a block of concrete, slumping, etc.), videotape is great. If you can, get hold of a cam-corder, some tape, and a VCR and observe yourself as you simulate entry, handshake, seating and interview.

When you have prepared yourself mentally and physically, you are ready for taking on your first interview. But there is one other item to remember: You may not get a job offer from every interview. Part of your preparation is to know how to deal with an unsuccessful effort, and probably the first lesson for you to learn is not to call it "failure." It is merely an unsuccessful effort from which you have learned a few things. These things will help you in your next interview.

If you use each interview as the springboard for the next interview until such time as you land a job that you want, you will be carrying your preparation over into the future, where it belongs as much as it does in the here and now.

In fact, the preparation that you do now will even help you once you are employed as a flight attendant by an airline of your choice. The same behavior that got you the job will help you keep it.

CHAPTER 9

Types of Interviews

You can face three different types of interview once you have begun your job search in earnest. You should be aware of all three kinds so that you can be ready for them, particularly since they involve such a diverse range of questions, designed to elicit a wide range of information from you.

Group Interview/Personnel Briefing

This kind of interview involves sometimes large groups of people and is used for initial screening. The size of the group being interviewed can be from five to 50 applicants. One or two company officials will conduct the interview. There usually will be a formal company introduction; then, in most cases, each applicant will be asked to stand, introduce herself or himself, and give a one- or two-minute synopsis of his or her background. Applicants may be required to conduct cross interviews of each other, then introduce their interviewees to the group.

Such an interview format may seem impersonal, but you should not give the interview any less than 100 percent effort. Types of questions the interviewers may ask include:

- Questions to individuals at random.

- Specific questions to particular individuals.

- The same question to all individuals.

In a group setting with a large number of applicants, the overall impact of each candidate is evaluated. Standard areas of evaluation:

- Are you neat and well-groomed?

- Are you attractive physically?

- Do you style your hair appropriately? Is the cut right?

- Is your complexion good?

- Are your teeth straight and white? Is your smile attractive?

- Are your hands and nails well-groomed?

- Is your posture good or bad?

- Are you self-confident?

- Are you polite? Do you show good manners?

- Is your personality warm? Do you seem interested?

- Are you punctual?

When dealing with a large group of applicants, a recruiter generally has little time to pursue each candidate individually, so appropriate questions that can be answered rather quickly are used to evaluate a candidate's communication skills, personality, intelligence, poise, initiative, grammar and voice tone. A few questions that may be asked:

- Why do you want to fly for our company?

- Why do you want to be a flight attendant?

- What type of work are you doing now?

- How does your family feel about your decision to pursue this career?

- What will make this job rewarding enough to leave your present position?

- What kind of recommendation will your present employer give you?

- How many times have you been absent from work in the past two years?

- What do you consider to be good attendance?

- What kind of flight attendant will be you be?

- What attributes do you have that will make you a good flight attendant?

- How do you feel about serving people?

Any candidate who exhibits inappropriate behavior, dress or appearance or who gives poor responses during the group session will probably be disqualified from consideration for the next level of interviewing and evaluation. You should prepare yourself to the degree that, when interview time arrives, you will be ready for almost any question the recruiter is likely to throw at you.

The questions asked of you and the others will relate directly or indirectly to the nature of the flight attendant position. In the daily life of a flight attendant, there are many positive things, but difficulties abound, too. The recruiter is trying to learn which people in the group are most likely to enjoy the positive aspects of flight attending and to be able to handle with aplomb the hassles, problems and crises. Therefore, you owe yourself the kind of preparation that takes into consideration both the positive and negative aspects of flight attending.

Very attractive aspects of the position include:

- The opportunity to meet new and interesting people every day.

- The chance to make new and lifelong friends.

- A schedule that is flexible in comparison with the nine to five grind.

- More time off than is forthcoming in most other jobs.

- The possibility of living in or being based at a variety of cities.

- Frequent travel to a multiplicity of places.

- The opportunity to travel all over the world at deep discounts for air transport and at lesser discounts for other major areas of expenditure (hotels, restaurants).

- Paid vacations, excellent benefits, attractive salaries.

- Nifty-looking uniforms that eliminate the necessity for extensive wardrobes.

Negative aspects include:

- No guarantee of being based at a city of choice. Some airlines require six to 12 months at the first base station before a transfer will be permitted.

- Reserve status from six months to five or more years, depending on many variables. Under reserve, a flight attendant is on call 24 hours a day during duty periods and can be called out at any time.

- A work day that may be 14 hours long or longer.

- The necessity of dealing with all kinds of people (ill, irate, demanding, irrational) and yet maintaining a positive, friendly attitude at all times.

- The absolute demand for punctuality and good attendance.

- The need to maintain good health regardless of exposure to extremes of weather and irregular hours.

- Strict regulations for appearance, including such personal areas as hair style and makeup.

FLIGHT ATTENDANT QUESTIONNAIRE

If you are applying for a position as a Flight Attendant, please fill out this questionnaire and return it with a completed Eastern application form. This questionnaire has been designed to give you an opportunity to express yourself more completely than a standard application would permit. In addition, your responses will provide us with meaningful and pertinent information on which to base our assessment of your application. The questions included herein are not intended in any way to function in a discriminatory manner to the disadvantage of any applicant. Please answer the questions fully and candidly. Thank you very much for your interest in Eastern Airlines.

Name: Hireme (LAST) Willa (FIRST) You (MIDDLE)

Address: 3972 Wing Lane Airport, GA 30321

Telephone: (200) 222-8222

Height: 5' 5 1/2" Weight: 120 Uncorrected Vision: 20/20

Corrected Vision: N/A Health: Excellent (GOOD, AVERAGE, POOR) Any Physical Limitations: None

Describe yourself in terms of both appearance and personality. I am an attractive, well groomed woman. I have a clear complexion and my weight is in proportion to my height. My most prized compliment comes from being considered healthy looking by others. I am well mannered, polite and concerned. I take pride in myself and my work. I treat people the way I want to be treated. I am the type of person that people find easy to talk to. I am frequently chosen as a confidante by my friends. I am an optimist which accounts for my resilient positive attitude. Overall, I am a well adjusted and mature individual.

Are you pleased with yourself as a person? Please explain. Yes. I feel that I am well established in life. I have been able to attain the goals which I have set for myself. I enjoy my personal and financial independence which I have gained through hard work and persistence. I look forward to new learning experiences and strive to improve myself personally & professionally.

How do you feel about being told exactly what kind of uniform you must wear? As a public representative of your airline, my uniform symbolizes the organization for which I work. I recognize the significance of wearing a uniform in situations requiring authority i.e. boarding, emergencies, etc.

Have you ever lived out on your own, away from home? Yes **If so, how long?** Six years.

Under what circumstances? My first experience living away from home was when I went to college. When I joined the work force, I moved away from home permanently. My decision had been discussed with my family and I had their support.

In what types of non-employment activities have you been involved? (Include social, service, hobbies, sports, academic, campus pursuits, contests, awards, etc.) Volunteer: A.I. Dupont Institute working with mentally and physically handicapped children; College: Muscular Dystrophy Fund Raising Drive, Chapel Choir, Area Council Committee. HS: Honor Roll, Debate Team, MD All State Choir, Newspaper Staff.

Have you ever been interviewed for a Flight Attendant position (with Eastern or another company) before? If so, give details including any reason(s) you believe you were not accepted. Yes. I was interviewed and hired by Capital Air in 1981. I am currently employed at Capital as a flight attendant on the DC-8 and DC-10. I am based in New York and work scheduled flights worldwide.

What have you done to prepare yourself for this specific position? I was raised in an aviation family and gained knowledge of the requirements for being a flight attendant. I know that with my flight attendant experience, public contact background, first aid training and language skill, I am well prepared for a flight attendant position.

The recruiter will be trying to draw from you responses that will illuminate your personality and adaptability as these relate to the positives and negatives of airline work. When you are asked a question, avoid a simple yes or no answer. Unduly short responses of any kind will not give the recruiter the information needed to evaluate you. Your answer to the recruiter's question should be couched to sell YOU to the airline.

In the group interview, you may be given a list of words and asked to rank them in the order of their importance to you. Afterwards, you will be asked to explain your choices to the group. Your poise and articulation will be observed closely.

Some companies will require that you complete a questionnaire using an essay format for your answers. Examples of essay questions:

- Explain, using specific examples, what you can do to make a customer return to XYZ Airlines.

- What is your definition of good service?

- Why do you want to be a flight attendant?

During this phase of the interview, you also may be given a series of tests, including language skills tests and both aptitude and personality tests. In most instances, the aptitude test will be graded immediately. If you do not pass, the interview will be over for you. Aptitude tests include such separate testing areas as mathematical ability, vocabulary, reasoning ability, and reading skills. Examples of each type of question appear on the next few pages.

The mathematical test is likely to include a measure of an applicant's ability to make change, e.g., If you sold two drinks at $2.25 each and the customer gave you $10.00, what would his/her change be? Another area of mathematical testing at some carriers is the ability to comprehend the conversion of time to the 24-hour clock, e.g., 11 p.m. is 2300 hours (12 hours through noon, plus 11 hours since then).

You should be prepared at this stage to be measured and weighed. If you do not meet weight requirements, you may or may not continue the interview, but you probably will not be invited back for the second phase. At some companies, not meeting the height requirement will disqualify you immediately, as well.

SAMPLE APTITUDE QUESTIONS

The following are samples of question types most frequently found on aptitude tests taken by flight attendant applicants. Try answering these questions now, and mark your answer by circling the letter preceding the answer you choose. You will find correct answers and explanations of the answers after the questions.

MATHEMATICAL ABILITY

1. The length of time from 8:23 a.m. to 2:53 p.m. is

   (A) 6 hours, 16 minutes
   (B) 6 hours, 30 minutes
   (C) 7 hours, 16 minutes
   (D) 6 hours, 40 minutes

2. Although the metric system has not been generally accepted in the United States and Canada, it is used in most parts of Europe and by scientists everywhere. Many American cars feature speedometers which show kilometers per hour. If you are required to drive 500 miles, and you know that one kilometer is approximately 5/8 of a mile, how many kilometers would you cover in that journey?

   (A) 625
   (B) 800
   (C) 850
   (D) 1,000

3. Two sailors traveled by bus from one point to another. The trip took 15 hours, and they left their point of origin at 8 a.m. What time did they arrive at their destination?

   (A) 11 a.m.
   (B) 10 p.m.
   (C) 11 p.m.
   (D) 12 a.m.

4. Gary went to the store and bought a toy harmonica for $1.95 and an instruction booklet for 35¢. He gave the clerk $2.50. How much change did Gary get?

   (A) 20¢
   (B) 25¢
   (C) 30¢
   (D) 15¢

5. A change purse contained 3 half dollars, 8 quarters, 7 dimes, 6 nickels and 9 pennies. Express in dollars and cents the total amount of money in the purse.

   (A) $3.78
   (B) $4.32
   (C) $3.95
   (D) $4.59

6. A student was planning a trip to Europe. She had a total of $700 available for expenses. If the plane ticket cost $372, how much money did she have left?

   (A) $338
   (B) $248
   (C) $438
   (D) $328

7. A group left on a trip at 8:50 a.m. and reached their destination at 3:30 p.m. How long, in hours and minutes, did the trip take?

(A) 3 hours, 10 minutes
(B) 4 hours, 40 minutes
(C) 5 hours, 10 minutes
(D) 6 hours, 40 minutes

8. If a plane travels 1,000 miles in 5 hours, 30 minutes, what is its average speed in miles per hour?

   (A) 181 9/11
   (B) 200
   (C) 215
   (D) 191 1/2

9. A boy deposited in his savings account the money he had saved during the summer. Find the amount of his deposit if he had 10 one-dollar bills, 9 half dollars, 8 quarters, 16 dimes, and 25 nickels.

   (A) $16.20
   (B) $17.42
   (C) $18.60
   (D) $19.35

10. How much time is there between 8:30 a.m. today and 3:15 a.m. tomorrow?

    (A) 17 3/4 hours
    (B) 18 2/3 hours
    (C) 18 1/2 hours
    (D) 18 3/4 hours

11. A man deposited a check for $1,000 to open an account. Shortly after that, he withdrew $941.20. How much did he have left in his account?

    (A) $56.72
    (B) $58.80
    (C) $59.09
    (D) $60.60

12. A woman bought a lamp for $37.50. She gave the clerk $40 How much change did she get?

    (A) $3.50
    (B) $2.50
    (C) $2.75
    (D) $3.25

13. A pilot bought a shirt for $18.95. He gave the clerk $20. How much change did the pilot get?

    (A) $2.05
    (B) $1.95
    (C) $1.05
    (D) $ .05

14. The minute hand fell off a watch but the watch continued to work accurately. What time was it when the hour hand was at the 17-minute mark?

    (A) 3:02
    (B) 3:12
    (C) 3:24
    (D) 4:17

15. A plane left New York at 3:30 p.m. EST and arrived in Los Angeles at 19:15 PST. How long did the flight take?

    (A) 7 hours, 15 minutes
    (B) 6 hours, 45 minutes
    (C) 5 hours, 45 minutes
    (D) 6 hours, 15 minutes

VOCABULARY

Directions: Choose the word that has most nearly the same meaning as the CAPITALIZED word.

1. PURCHASE
   (A) charge
   (B) supply
   (C) order
   (D) buy

2. MANUAL
   (A) self-acting
   (B) simple
   (C) hand-operated
   (D) handmade

3. DEPORTMENT
   (A) attendance
   (B) intelligence
   (C) neatness
   (D) behavior

4. EXHIBIT
   (A) display
   (B) trade
   (C) sell
   (D) label

5. CAPTIVE
   (A) savage
   (B) jailer
   (C) spy
   (D) prisoner

6. VEGETATION
   (A) food
   (B) plant life
   (C) moisture
   (D) bird life

7. COMPETENT
   (A) busy
   (B) capable
   (C) friendly
   (D) good-natured

8. SUSPEND
   (A) turn back
   (B) check carefully
   (C) regulate strictly
   (D) stop temporarily

9. VACANT
   (A) quiet
   (B) stupid
   (C) available
   (D) empty

10. INCREDIBLE
    (A) thrilling
    (B) convincing
    (C) interesting
    (D) unbelievable

11. LEISURELY
    (A) roundabout
    (B) unhurried
    (C) unforgetable
    (D) tiresome

12. COMPREHEND
    (A) hear
    (B) listen
    (C) agree
    (D) understand

13. CONCLUSION
    (A) theme
    (B) suspense
    (C) end
    (D) beginning

14. AROMA
    (A) flavor
    (B) warmth
    (C) fragrance
    (D) steam

15. HAZARD
    (A) damage
    (B) choice
    (C) opportunity
    (D) danger

REASONING ABILITY

Directions: The first two words are related to each other in a certain way. The third and fourth words must be related to each other in the same way. Choose from among the four choices the word that is related to the third word in the same way that the second word is related to the first.

1. BOSS: FOREMAN :: PRESIDENT:
    (A) manager
    (B) employee
    (C) nation
    (D) congress

2. NECKLACE: BEAD :: CHAIN:
    (A) ball
    (B) link
    (C) iron
    (D) necklace

3. SCISSORS: CUT :: PEN:
    (A) point
    (B) ink
    (C) sty
    (D) write

4. HAND: BODY :: STAR:
    (A) sky
    (B) universe
    (C) eye
    (D) movie

5. EGG: BEAT :: POTATO:
    (A) yam
    (B) bake
    (C) eye
    (D) mash

6. SKILLFUL: CLUMSY :: DEFT:
    (A) alert
    (B) awkward
    (C) dumb
    (D) agile

7. SMALL: MINIATURE :: LARGE:
    (A) dwarf
    (B) big
    (C) cameo
    (D) gigantic

8. HEAT: RADIATOR :: BREEZE:
    (A) sea
    (B) wind
    (C) shade
    (D) fan

9. DAY: NIGHT :: SUN:
    (A) solar
    (B) moon
    (C) daylight
    (D) heat

10. DOG: CANINE :: CAT:
    (A) bovine
    (B) tiger
    (C) feminine
    (D) feline

11. PIG: PORK :: STEER:
    (A) cow
    (B) ranch
    (C) beef
    (D) pony

12. WINDOW: PANE :: DOOR:
    (A) sill
    (B) lock
    (C) key
    (D) bell

13. SEAL: FISH :: BIRD:
    (A) wing
    (B) minnow
    (C) worm
    (D) snail

14. BED: SLEEP :: CHAIR:
    (A) carry
    (B) sit
    (C) stare
    (D) awake

15. SURGEON : SCALPEL :: BUTCHER:
    (A) meat
    (B) cleaver
    (C) wrench
    (D) beef

READING SKILLS

Directions: Choose the most appropriate answer for each of the following questions.

1. Prior to the Civil War, the steamboat was the center of life in the thriving Mississippi towns. With the war came the railroads. River traffic dwindled and the white-painted vessels rotted at the wharves. During World War I, the government decided to relieve rail congestion by reviving the long-forgotten waterways. Today, steamers, diesels and barges ply the Mississippi.

   The paragraph best supports the statement that

   (A) the volume of river transportation was greater than the volume of rail transportation during World War I.
   (B) growth of river transportation greatly increased the congestion on the railroads.
   (C) business found river transportation more profitable than railroad transportation during World War I.
   (D) since the Civil War, the volume of transportation on the Mississippi has varied.

2. Specialization could not exist without the process of exchange. A farmer might specialize in

raising corn. In the course of a year he would produce many more bushels of corn than he and his family could possibly consume. However, being a specialist, he can neither grow the other foods he needs, nor produce such necessities of life as clothing, shelter, newspapers and machinery. What he does, in effect, is exchange his corn for those products.

As a result of specialization

(A) the process of exchange has been greatly accelerated.
(B) the farm has become a business.
(C) the farmer's produce must be sent to the open market for distribution.
(D) food products become the specialized field of the farmer.

3. There exists a false but popular idea that a clue is a mysterious fact that most people overlook but which some very keen investigator easily discovers and recognizes as having, in itself, a remarkable meaning. The clue is most often an ordinary fact that an observant person picks up — something that gains its significance when, after a long series of careful investigations, it is connected with a network of other clues.

To be of value clues must be

(A) discovered by skilled investigators.
(B) found under mysterious circumstances.
(C) connected with other facts.
(D) discovered soon after the crime.

4. It was formerly thought that whole wheat and graham breads were far superior to white bread made from highly refined wheat flour. However, it is now believed that the general use of milk solids in white bread significantly narrows the nutritional gap between the two types of bread. About the only dietary advantages now claimed for whole wheat bread are higher content of iron and vitamin B, both easily obtainable in many other common foods.

The paragraph best supports the statement that

(A) white bread is fattening because of its milk content.
(B) whole wheat bread is not much more nutritious than white bread.
(C) whole wheat bread contains roughage.
(D) white bread contains neither iron nor vitamin B.

5. Economy once in a while is just not enough. I expect to find it at every level of responsibility, from cabinet member to the newest

and youngest recruit. Controlling waste is something like bailing a boat; you have to keep at it. I have no intention of easing up on my insistence on getting a dollar of value for each dollar we spend.

The paragraph best supports the statement that

(A) we need not be concerned about items which cost less than a dollar.
(B) it is advisable to buy the cheaper of two items.
(C) the responsibility of economy is greater at high levels than at low levels.
(D) economy is a continuing responsibility.

6. Scientists have learned a great deal about the huge animals that lived millions of years ago from clues found in rocks. These clues are called fossils. There are many kinds of fossils. They may be footprints found in mud hardened to rock, or they may be bones or teeth found thousands of years after an animal has died.

The best interpretation of the passage is that

(A) a clue is a fossil.
(B) mud becomes as hard as rock when it ages.
(C) someday we may all be fossils.
(D) we know much about early life on this earth from fossils.

7. In almost every community, fortunately, there are certain men and women known to be public-spirited. Others, however, may be selfish and act only as their private interests seem to require.

The paragraph suggests that those citizens who disregard others are

(A) needed.
(B) found only in small communities.
(C) not known.
(D) not public-spirited.

8. Many people think that only older men who have a great deal of experience should hold public office. These people lose sight of an important fact. Many of the founding fathers of our country were comparatively young men. Today more than ever our country needs young, idealistic politicians.

The best interpretation of what this author believes is that

(A) only experienced men should hold public office.
(B) only idealistic men should hold public office.
(C) younger men can and should take part in politics.
(D) young people don't like politics.

9. It is a common assumption that city directories are prepared and published by the cities concerned. However, the directory business is as much a private business as is the publishing of dictionaries and encyclopedias. The companies financing the publication make their profits through the sales of the directories themselves and through the advertising in them.

The paragraph best supports the statement that

(A) the publication of a city directory is a commercial enterprise.
(B) the size of a city directory limits the space devoted to advertising.
(C) many city directories are published by dictionary and encyclopedia concerns.
(D) city directories are sold at cost to local residents and businessmen.

10. The view is widely held that butter is more digestible and better absorbed than other fats because of its low melting point. There is little scientific authority for such a view. As margarine is made today, its melting point is close to that of butter, and tests show only the slightest degree of difference in digestibility of fats of equally low melting points.

The paragraph best supports the statement that

(A) butter is more easily digested than margarine.
(B) there is not much difference in the digestibility of butter and margarine.
(C) most people prefer butter to margarine.
(D) it sometimes becomes necessary to use a substitute for butter.

11. The indiscriminate or continual use of any drug without medical supervision is dangerous. Even drugs considered harmless may result in chronic poisoning if used for a period of years. Prescriptions should not be refilled without consulting your doctor. He prescribed a given amount because he wished to limit your use of the drug to a certain time. Never use a drug prescribed for someone else just because your symptoms appear similar. There may be differences, apparent to an expert but hidden from you, which indicate an entirely different ailment requiring different medication.

The paragraph best supports the statement that

(A) the use of drugs is very dangerous.
(B) if a physician prescribes a drug it is safe to refill the prescription.
(C) people with similar symptoms are usually

suffering from the same ailment.
(D) a drug considered harmless may be dangerous if taken over a long period of time without supervision.

12. The coloration of textile fabrics composed of cotton and wool generally requires two processes, as the process used in dyeing wool is seldom capable of fixing the color upon cotton. The usual method is to immerse the fabric in the requisite baths to dye the wool and then to test the partially dyed material in the manner found suitable for cotton.

   The dyeing of textile fabrics composed of cotton and wool

   (A) is more successful when the material contains more cotton than wool.
   (B) is not satisfactory when solid colors are desired
   (C) is restricted to two colors for any one fabric.
   (D) is based upon the methods required for dyeing the different materials.

13. Most solids, like most liquids, expand when heated and contract when cooled. To allow for this, roads, sidewalks and railroad tracks are constructed with spacing between sections so that they can expand during the hot weather.

   If roads, sidewalks and railroad tracks were not constructed with spacings between sections

   (A) nothing would happen to them when the weather changed.
   (B) they could not be constructed as easily as they are now.
   (C) they would crack or break when the weather changed.
   (D) they would not appear to be even.

14. Certain chemical changes, such as fermentation, are due to the action of innumerable living microorganisms known as bacteria. Bacteria also cause the decomposition of sewage.

   Certain chemical changes are due to

   (A) bacteria.
   (B) oxidation.
   (C) fermentation.
   (D) decomposition.

15. Foreign-born adults hold on to the habits, preferences and loyalties of their homelands. Their speech, if they learn English at all, reflects the accent and idiom of their land of origin. Children, on the other hand,

acquire English without a trace of accent and, through their playmates and school life, learn to prefer American clothing and mannerisms to the customs and dress of their parents.

Which of the following statements best summarizes the paragraph?

(A) American customs are more complicated than the customs of other countries.
(B) Foreign-born children become Americanized more quickly than their parents.
(C) Immigrant children do not respect their parents.
(D) It is nearly impossible for foreigners to adopt American ways.

Answers to Sample Aptitude Questions

MATHEMATICAL ABILITY

1. **(B)** Convert to a 24-hour clock. 2:53 p.m. = 14.53

   14:53
   -8:23
   6:30 = 6 hours, 30 minutes

2. **(B)** Convert the miles to kilometers by dividing them by ⁵/₈.

   500 miles ÷ ⁵/₈ = $\frac{500}{1} \times \frac{8}{5}$ = $\frac{100}{1} \times \frac{8}{1}$ = 800 kilometers

3. **(C)** 8 a.m. + 15 hours = 23 o'clock = 11 p.m.

4. **(A)** Gary paid $1.95 + $.35 = $2.30
   $2.50 - $2.30 = $.20

5. **(D)** $ .50 x 3 = $ 1.50
   .25 x 8 = $ 2.00
   + .10 x 7 = $ .70
   .05 x 6 = $ .30
   .01 x 9 = $ .09
   ─────────────
   $ 4.59

6. **(D)** $700 - $372 = $328

7. **(D)** First convert to a 24 hour clock. 3:30 p.m. = 15:30 o'clock
   15:30 = 14:90
   - 8:50 = 8:50
   ─────────────────
   6:40 = 6 hrs. 40 min.

   To subtract a larger number of minutes from a smaller number of minutes, borrow 60 minutes from the hour to enlarge the smaller number.

8. **(A)** 5 hours, 30 minutes = 5 ½ hours
1000 mph ÷ 5 ½ hours
$= 1000 \div {}^{11}/_2 = 1000 \times {}^2/_{11} = 181 \, {}^9/_{11}$ m.p.h.

9. **(D)**
    10 x $1.00 = $10.00
     9 x .50 = $4.50
     8 x .25 = 2.00
    16 x .10 = 1.60
    25 x .05 = 1.25
                     $19.35

10. **(D)** From 8:30 a.m.   12:00 = 11:60
    until noon today: - 8:30 = 8:30
                                  3 hrs. 30 min.
    from noon until midnight: + 12 hrs.
    from midnight to 3:15 a.m.:   3 hrs. 15 min.
                                  18 hrs. 45 min. = 18 ¾ hrs.

11. **(B)** $1,000 - $941.20 = $58.80

12. **(B)** $40 - $37.50 = $2.50

13. **(C)** $20 - $18.95 = $1.05

14. **(C)** Visualize the face of the clock. When the hour hand is at the 17-minute mark it is between the 3 and the 4, so the time is somewhat after 3:00 o'clock. 17 is approximately ⅔ of the way between the 3 and the 4 (between 15 and 20), 3:24 is the most accurate guess.

15. **(B)** PST (Pacific Standard Time) is three hours earlier than EST (Eastern Standard Time), so to figure actual trip time you must add three hours to the given arrival time. Arrival at 19:15 PST is equivalent to arrival at 22:15 EST. 22:15 is 10:15 p.m. The time from 3:30 p.m. to 10:15 p.m. is 6 hours, 45 minutes.

VOCABULARY

1. **(D)** To *purchase* is to *buy* for a price.

2. **(C)** *Manual*, as opposed to automatic or mechanical, means *hand-operated*.

3. **(D)** *Deportment* means *behavior* or *conduct*.

4. **(A)** To *exhibit* means to *show publicly* or to *display*. Often one exhibits goods which one hopes to subsequently trade or sell.

5. **(D)** The *captive* is the one who was *captured* and made *prisoner*, regardless of the reason for his capture.

6. **(B)** The term *vegetation* includes all *plant life*.

7. **(B)** *Competent* means *qualified* or *capable*.

8. **(D)** To *suspend* is to *stop temporarily*.

9. **(D)** *Vacant* means *unfilled* or *empty*.

10. **(D)** That which is *incredible* is *too improbable to believe*.

11. **(B)** *Leisure* is *freedom from pressure*. With no time pressure, a vacation can be leisurely or unhurried.

12. **(D)** To *comprehend* is to *grasp the meaning of* or to *understand*.

13. **(C)** The *conclusion* is the *end*.

14. **(C)** An *aroma* is a *pleasing smell* or *fragrance*.

15. **(D)** A *hazard* is a *risk, peril*, or *danger*.

REASONING ABILITY

1. **(A)** The relationship is pretty much that of synonym or definition. The BOSS is the FOREMAN; the PRESIDENT is a MANAGER. The *president* may manage *employees* of a company; the *president* may manage the *nation* and may try to manage *Congress*, but that relationship is one of actor to object, which is not the relationship expressed by the original pair.

2. **(B)** The relationship is that of the whole to one of its parts. NECKLACE is the whole of which a BEAD is a part; CHAIN is a whole of which a LINK is a part. A *chain* may be made of *iron*, but it then would be analogous to a relationship such as "necklace:glass" in which the second term describes the composition of the first.

3. **(D)** The analogy is one of function or purpose. SCISSORS CUT; a PEN WRITES.

4. **(B)** The relationship is that of the part to the whole. A HAND is part of the BODY; a STAR is in the *sky*, but it is part of the UNIVERSE.

5. **(D)** The relationship is that of object to action. When one BEATS an EGG, one performs a violent act upon the substance of the *egg*. When one MASHES a POTATO, one performs an analogous act upon the *potato*. Baking the potato prepares it for eating, but the act of *baking* is not analogous to the act of *beating*. If *mash* were not offered as a choice, *bake* might have served as the answer. You must always choose the *best* answer available.

6. **(B)** The analogy is one of opposites or antonyms. CLUMSY is the opposite of SKILLFUL; AWKWARD is the opposite of DEFT. *Agile* is a synonym for *deft*.

7. **(D)** The analogy is one of degree. MINIATURE is very, very SMALL; GIGANTIC is very, very LARGE.

8. **(D)** The relationship is that of the effect to its cause. Both *wind* and a *fan* can cause a *breeze*, so you must further refine the relationship. *Artificial* HEAT is produced by a RADIATOR; an *artificial* BREEZE is produced by a FAN.

9. **(B)** The relationship of DAY to NIGHT is clearly that of opposites. In the same way SUN and MOON are opposites.

10. **(D)** The relationship is that of part to whole. DOG is a member of the zoological family CANINE; CAT is a member of the zoological family FELINE. *Tiger* is also a member of the *feline* family. The relationship of *tiger* to *cat* is part to part. *Bovine* is another zoological family, which includes cows.

11. **(C)** PIG is the source of PORK; STEER is the source of BEEF. *Steer* is the male animal while *cow* is the female animal. A *steer* may live on a *ranch*.

12. **(B)** The relationship is that of the whole to its part. WINDOW is the larger object of which a PANE is a part; DOOR is the larger object of which a LOCK is a part. The *sill* is an integral part of the door assembly, but it is not a part of the *door* itself. A *key* has an important functional relationship with both *door* and *lock*, but it is not part of the door.

13. **(C)** The relationship is that of actor to object or, if you like, eater to eaten. A SEAL eats FISH; a BIRD eats WORMS.

14. **(B)** The relationship is one of function or purpose. A BED is to SLEEP on; a CHAIR is to SIT on. *Awake*, (D), is not the correct answer because it fails to maintain grammatical parallelism. "Chair:awake" would be a correct completion if the initial pair had read "bed:asleep."

15. **(B)** This is a purpose relationship. A SURGEON uses a SCALPEL in the practice of his trade; a BUTCHER uses a CLEAVER in the practice of his trade. The *butcher* might use a *wrench* in repairing a meat grinder, but that use would be incidental rather than central to his everyday work.

READING SKILLS

1. **(D)** The paragraph describes the varied history of Mississippi River traffic. Before the advent of the railroads, the river was the chief avenue of commerce. When the railroads took over, the river fell into disuse. Use of the river was revived when the railroads became overburdened by traffic. The other three answer choices all contradict the facts stated in the paragraph.

2. **(A)** Since "specialization could not exist without the process of exchange," the process of exchange has been greatly accelerated as a result of specialization. People who specialize in producing or growing one particular necessity must exchange their own products for other necessities.

3. **(C)** The paragraph tells us that the value of a clue lies in its relationship to all the other clues.

4. **(B)** The point of the paragraph is that fortified white bread is nearly as nutritious as whole wheat bread.

5. **(D)** See the first sentence.

6. **(D)** The first sentence states that we have learned much about life on earth from fossils.

7. **(D)** The connective "others, however," with which the second sentence begins implies the converse of the first. Some citizens are public-spirited; others, however, are not.

8. **(C)** The last sentence states that the country needs young, idealistic politicians.

9. **(A)** The business of publishing city directories is a private business operated for profit. As such, it is a commercial enterprise.

10. **(B)** As far as digestibility is concerned, there is little difference between butter and margarine because they have

11. **(D)** The second sentence answers the question perfectly.

12. **(D)** The paragraph tells us that the dyeing of wool requires a process quite different from that for dyeing cotton. Fabric which contains both wool and cotton fibers must go through both processes, one after the other.

13. **(C)** The spaces allow roads, sidewalks, and railroad tracks to expand in summer and contract in winter without cracking or breaking.

14. **(A)** Fermentation and decomposition are chemical changes brought about by the action of bacteria.

15. **(B)** Although foreign-born adults hold on to their old ways, children adapt to the language, clothing, and mannerisms of their playmates. In other words, the children become Americanized more quickly than their parents.

PERSONALITY TESTING

There are a number of psychological/personality tests in common use. These tend to ask you to describe yourself by choosing which statements apply to you, by answering questions about your attitudes and likes and dislikes, or by rating yourself on a continuum of traits and then predicting how others might rate you. Psychological/personality tests are usually very long. The length of the test allows for internal controls against your trying to create an impression. The length also assures that no single answer carries undue weight.

One of the most frequently used tests is the Minnesota Multiphasic Personality Inventory, known as the MMPI. This test consists of 560 statements to which candidates must answer "true" or "false." Some examples of MMPI items:

I like school.
I like to cook.
Someone is trying to poison me.
I like to tease animals.
I would rather win than lose in a game.
I do not like everyone I know.
I am not afraid of mice.

I like repairing a door latch.
I dread the thought of an earthquake.
My parents have often objected to the kind of people I went around with.

There are no right or wrong answers. Simply answer honestly. The total pattern of answers paints a picture of your personality and helps the airline to decide if you would be happy and successful as a flight attendant.

Personal Interview/One-on-One

After you pass the initial stages of the interview process, you will be invited for another session to explore you as a candidate, with the focus on the inner you.

"Screening/Initial Impact," as this session is called, usually begins with the question, "Tell me about yourself." Your answer should be organized, chronological, well-delivered, and expressive of a rounded picture of yourself.

The interviewer continually evaluates you on a point system. An applicant can make points (a plus), fail to make points (a minus), or lose points (a minus). Conclusions from an interview are based on the assumption that the past and the present are auguries of the future. Personnel representatives are looking for appearance, flexibility, job knowledge, sociability, sensitivity to others, communication skills, desire to learn and grow, work ethic, and attitude.

If you can prepare yourself for questions pertaining to the following issues — understanding, as you put together your responses, how the questions will be designed to explore your character and personality in relation to the flight attendant profile — then you will be able to project poise, confidence and self-esteem.

Following are dimensions of the total you that will be explored during your personal interview:

- Impact. This category involves physical and facial characteristics; complexion; teeth and smile; neatness and grooming; demeanor (are you self-confident?); politeness and manners; and amount of warmth and interest.

- Oral communication. Interviewer evaluates fluency; eye contact; grammar; relevancy and logic of responses and comments; enthusiasm and sincerity.

- Energy/stress tolerance. Evaluated are your self-assurance; whether or not you exhibit excessive nervousness or distracting mannerisms; your past ability to handle responsibility, as displayed through your work experience; and your participation in activities (job-related or otherwise) requiring physical effort.

- Prior work record. Examined are absenteeism; reasons for leaving previous jobs; whether previous employers will give a positive recommendation; your performance standards; and significant personal projects in which you may have been involved.

When you meet with an interviewer on a one-to-one basis, you can be assured of being allotted at least 20 minutes of time in which to sell yourself.

This interview may follow directly upon the group interview, or you may be invited back for this one-on-one meeting. The interview is conducted by a personnel representative, and your paperwork (employment application, resume, other forms) will be checked at this time. The length of the interview will depend on how well you interact with the interviewer.

All questions during this interview will be specific; your answers will tell the company about you as an individual. Questions will be designed to solicit more than a yes or no answer. If the company is conducting separate screening interviews, be prepared to have your height and weight checked again (airlines want to be sure that they will not have to worry about a weight fluctuation problem). Collect yourself mentally and physically, silently outline your major thoughts, then speak them, projecting warmth and enthusiasm in your voice. Exit the interview with a smile, confident and poised.

Commonly Asked Interview Questions

What do you think of labor unions?
Have you interviewed with other companies?
Why do you want to work for our company?
To what other companies have you applied?
What is a good flight attendant?
What is your philosophy of life?

What is a good friend?
What would you change in your life?
What was the last book you read and why?
How did you decide what college to attend?
Tell us about your grades in college.
Does your family mind moving?
What makes a good parent?
Why do you feel you are a good candidate for this position?
What is your definition of professionalism?
Tell us what you know about this company.
What does your spouse think of you?
What are your outside interests?
What do you think of the people you work with?
How did you arrange time for this interview?
What are your career plans as a flight attendant?
Use three adjectives to describe yourself.
Can you live on our starting salary?
What are your career and personal goals for five years from now?

Personal Interview/Board or Panel

This third type of interview is conducted by a panel of three or more interviewers, with you as the sole interviewee. The interviewers will take turns asking you questions and observing you.

You may be asked to read an in-flight announcement using a microphone. You may be asked situational questions, i.e., "What would you do if . . . ?" You also may be asked to role-play in a situation.

At this interview phase, the level of competition and of stress rises. Your reaction to a battery of questions will be observed closely. Answer the questions one at a time.

Remain calm. Ask the interviewer to repeat a question if necessary. Remember, this kind of interview is designed to observe you under stress.

When answering questions, bear in mind the following advice, extracted from *Sweaty Palms, The Neglected Art of Being Interviewed*, by H. Anthony Medley:

- The most important [thing] that an interviewer gets out of an interview is a subjective feeling about the interviewee. You must enhance that feeling.

- If the question is ambiguous, you should either interpret it in your way and say what puts you in the best light or ask for a clarification.

- Use ploys to get thinking time; ask for a clarification or use a bridge.

- Don't worry about thinking for a few seconds before you answer.

- Act natural.

- Assume that every question is asked for a purpose.

- Be ready for the blockbuster question.

- Handle the offensive question firmly but tactfully.

- Don't talk against a former employer.

- If you must discuss a bad situation [that you had] with a former employer, do so dispassionately.

- Answer specific questions specifically.

- Don't respond to a serious question with a flip joke.

- If you joke, don't make the interviewer the butt of it.

- Recognize dual-purpose questions and answer them decisively.

Plumbing Your Depths

You will be surprised at how deeply the interview process probes into your life, your mind, your personality, your character.

Using a flight attendant profile as a guide, the interviewers, throughout all levels of interviewing, will be exploring your motivation and aptitude for public contact work; your sensitivity to others; your energy level; your work standards; your initiative; your educational background; and your adaptability.

View all questions positively, as a chance to show the kind of stuff of which you are made. Following are specific questions that you will encounter at various stages of the hiring process. They are designed to induce you to paint a self-portrait.

Motivation and aptitude for public contact work

You will have a chance to portray how well you have worked with others in previous situations and will be able to express your personal satisfaction in working with and serving the needs of other people. You also will have an opportunity to give realistic reasons for seeking the flight attendant position and to display no reluctance about accepting the responsibilities and lifestyle of flight attending.

Questions frequently asked:

- What do you like most about your present job?

- What do you like least?

- What is most satisfying about your present job? The least satisfying? Can you give examples?

- Aside from company benefits and travel advantages, what makes the flight attendant position attractive to you?

- In what ways do you see this position as being similar to anything that you've ever done before?

- What would be the easiest part of the flight attendant job for you? The most challenging?

- Where do you see yourself five years from now?

- How would your friends describe you?

- What experiences in the recent past have been particularly rewarding for you?

Sensitivity to others

These responses can indicate that you are aware of the needs and feelings of others at work or on a personal level. Questions may include:

- Can you think of any problems you personally have caused others?

- Describe a situation where you encountered an angry person.

- What did you do and how did it help the situation?

- What problems have you encountered with customers or fellow employees? How did you handle them?

- If you had your choice, what kind of position would you like most to have?

- What type of passenger would you most like to have?

Energy level

Flight attending is an active profession that requires a great deal of vitality. You have decided already that you have the energy needed to be a flight attendant. Now you have to sell the company on this aspect of yourself. Questions exploring your energy level may include:

- What extracurricular activities are you involved in? What club offices have you held?

- Are they worth the time you devote to them?

- What are your leisure-time activities? Hobbies?

- Do you keep in good physical condition?

- Do you enjoy sports as an observer or as a participant?

- Can you work well under stress?

Work standards

This category of question and response indicates your willingness to take responsibility at work; the quality of work that you do; and your punctuality, attitude, dependability and attendance. Always try to accentuate the positive. Do not leave any gaps in employment unexplained. If there was a problem with a past employer, here is your chance to explain while you have someone who wants to listen. Questions include:

- Why did you leave your past employment?

- Tell me about your job history.

- What is a typical day like for you at work?

- In your present position, how do you define doing a good job?

- How did your previous employers treat you?

- Describe something that you've done that shows initiative at work.

- What would your present/past employer say about your job performance?

- Is there anything you were trying to improve about your job performance?

- How many days were you absent from work in the past year? Why?

- Were there some policies that you were asked to follow that you didn't agree with? How did you handle that?

Initiative

Your answers to this type of question will show whether you are passive in reacting to events or whether you actively try to shape events.

- Have you found any ways to make your present job more rewarding?

- Describe a situation, either personal or in your present job, where you were not satisfied with the way things were going and what you did to make things better.

- Can you give an example of an instance in which you anticipated problems and took action to prevent them?

- What type of passenger would you find most challenging in this job?

- How do you react when others lose their temper or become upset?

Educational background

These questions will help the interviewer establish how committed you were to school work. The responses to these questions will give you a chance to talk about your education. You should convey a sense of stability and maturity.

- What subjects did you like best in school? Least?

- [For those with a college background:] If you could start your college education over, would you change your major? What would you change it to and why?

- What was your grade point average?

- How did you finance your education?

Adaptability

Since the flight attendant position requires sacrifices in the beginning, interviewers will be curious about your ability to be flexible. The job probably will require that you move away from home, family and friends. Questions will explore your past flexibility and how well you conform to company policies and rules. Examples of questions:

- Have you ever lived away from home? What problems did you encounter in making adjustments?

- Have you ever been asked to follow rules that you did not like? What were they? What did you do?

- Have you ever felt that a boss habitually gave you the wrong orders? Why did you feel that way?

- Have you ever had a problem with the schedule you had to work? What was the schedule like? Did you ever miss work because of your problems with it?

CHAPTER 10

The Day of Your Interview

All of your planning for the interview that is only a few hours away can either pay off or be in vain, depending on how well you take care of practical details.

A favorable first impression on your prospective airline employer may depend on your being prepared for difficulties; in remembering to take along all of the items that you will need; in locating the place of the interview; in handling yourself in the reception area; and in other equally "insignificant" details.

Be On Time

Some employers have already made up their minds not to hire anybody who is not punctual in showing up for the interview. Even a minute late could mean that you drove or flew to the interview in vain.

If the interview is in your home town, make sure you know where the interview will be held. It is not always at the airport or in the airline's employment office; it could be in the meeting room of a local hotel. Read carefully all of the material that is sent to you regarding the day of the interview. You are not alone if you do not know every section of your home town in detail (you most likely are alone if you do); if you are not sure of the location of the address given, calling the airline for directions is perfectly acceptable. You then might take the added precaution of making a trial drive to the location, checking out an alternate route in case of traffic problems. Time your drive to make sure that you will arrive early enough to collect your thoughts before being called in for your interview.

How much time is the minimum for gathering your composure and collecting your thoughts? Only you can tell for sure — but 15 minutes is the absolute minimum that most people need in a situation like this one. If you are exceptionally early, you can always go to a coffee shop or other facility and relax. This device will get you out of the way of other company business and will avoid the risk that you might appear overly anxious while waiting in the reception area. This 30- or 40-minute quiet time is a far better way for the first part of your visit to go than for you to arrive at the last possible moment rushed, flustered, and quite likely already perspiring heavily from stress.

If you are late through causes truly beyond your control, you must have a valid explanation to offer. Not being able to find the office never has been an adequate excuse, and it will not be in your case, either. If you have had an accident, telephone the office as soon as possible to let your interviewer know what happened to you. Express how truly sorry you are and ask to be rescheduled if this is practicable. If the recruiter or interviewer cannot be reached, write a letter of apology immediately, explaining succinctly and asking to be rescheduled.

Prepared, Equipped and Alone

If a family member or friend wants to come with you, find a comfortable place where he or she can wait for you. Never bring anyone along to the employment office waiting room with you. You must project the confidence indicating that you can do the job without needing continual doses of moral support.

You will need your "interview tools," which include:

- Pen, pencil and paper (the pen should be a nice, professional-looking tool in keeping with the image you want to project)

- Extra copies of your resume
- A list of references, complete with addresses
- Extra photographic prints of yourself
- Social Security card
- Doctor's certificate, if necessary
- A neat folder or well-organized briefcase in which to carry all of the above
- An umbrella or raincoat if it is raining

There appear to be pros and cons attached to note taking during an interview. In a group interview, you will have more freedom to take notes. This interview is in large part an information session, and since there are more applicants than interviewers present, you will not be expected to maintain the more or less continuous eye contact that is demanded in a one-on-one or panel-on-one interview.

Note taking in either of the latter two situations is virtually impossible (considerable aplomb is required to pull off this piece of impertinence); it runs counter to your overriding goal, which is to sell yourself to the interviewers; and interviewers, without exception, would rather have you paying attention to the interrelationships and issues of the interview than to a note pad.

In situations where common sense or common courtesy dictates that you not take notes, do not take them; after the session is over, while everything is still fresh in your mind, is the time for note taking.

The reason for bringing along extra copies of your resume is that airline employment offices deal in large volumes of paperwork and sometimes cannot locate an applicant's file. If your resume has been misplaced, your extra copies will come in handy.

Do not be one of those pushy people who insist on attaching a resume or computer printout of "highlights" to the application form if you are asked to fill one out at some time during your visit. If company personnel explain that the application elicits all of the information about your qualifications that they will need, believe them; they will not look kindly upon deliberate disregard of their instructions.

Bring photographs for the same reason that you bring a couple of extra copies of your resume. Any pictures should be professionally done unless you are able to do them at home in a "professional-looking" setting. One full-length

On Being a Star

One aspect of presenting yourself during an interview has not been covered in any detail as yet. It involves your response to the pressure to which you will be subjected, particularly the extra pressure generated by certain of the questions you will be asked.

The category of question alluded to is a type for which the only real preparation is self-reliance, but you can improve your chances by being aware of what questions are asked and why.

The category? Stress questions.

Stress questions are designed to learn how well you know yourself, how well you understand the company product, and how willing you are to make the sacrifices that a new flight attendant is required to make. Failure to answer this type of question effectively could ruin your chances of being hired.

Although there is no script to follow when responding to these questions, the most important rule is to be absolutely honest. Disingenuousness or deception will always come back to hurt you at some point.

However, here as elsewhere, you should offer positives rather than negatives about yourself. Being able, for example, to recount a situation in which you have learned something positive from a negative experience may be regarded as showing maturity and integrity.

Following are some typical stress questions:

- Why should we hire you?

- Where do you see yourself in five years?

- What are your strengths and weaknesses?

- What did you like most (or least) about your last job?

- Why are you leaving your present position?

- Have you ever had a problem in dealing with a fellow employee or a boss?

For the first of these questions, do not be afraid to use up a few minutes of the interviewer's time giving a brief synopsis of "why you should hire me." This question is a wonderful opportunity for you to reiterate your assessment of your assets, goals, stability, experience, loyalty, and pride in representing this company if they should hire you. Do not hesitate to be proud of your accomplishments. As in a good sales presentation, always finish with a strong close.

As for where you see yourself five years in the future: Take this question as an opportunity to state your goals. If management is your goal, say so. If you feel you may want to make a career of flying, let the interviewers know how you feel. At the same time, try not to appear too pushy about climbing the airline ladder too quickly. Starting from the bottom takes some time.

Remember: Wanting to learn to be the best in your job is a commendable quality.

You know best how to prepare yourself for a "strengths vs. weaknesses" question. Just be sure that you prepare an answer in advance to this kind of question. Weaknesses can work in your favor if you are able to tell your interviewer how you have overcome them: "I am . . . but I have tried to overcome this fault by. . . ."

As noted earlier, you should never denigrate or blame your current or a former employer for any situations that may have arisen. Keep everything positive. The interviewers are trying to find out if you have been prone to conflicts with or resentments toward the people for whom you have worked in the past. The same holds true for your relations with fellow employees on past jobs. If you feel you may get an unfavorable reference from a previous employer, explain the situation, but make your explanation as understanding and positive as possible.

Another no-no: Never challenge the person or persons interviewing you, and never put one of them on the spot. A good rapport with your interviewer is a must.

One of the questions an interviewer can really put you on the spot with is "Are you overqualified for this position?" It is in a way an unfair question, since the more education you have and the broader your experience in dealing with people, the better you should compare with your competition. However, the interviewer wants to see how you handle this question, so if the basis for this challenge is extensive experience that you have in some other field, use that experience as an argument in your favor. The concern of the employer is that you may become bored with flight attending if you have had extensive experience in a challenging and rewarding field other than airline work. Make your answer dispel such doubts.

Following are some "stress question" factors that could disqualify you if your responses are not appropriate:

- Lack of job goals and focus. Know what is important to you and learn how to express it in a concise, intelligent statement: "I want to . . . for your company as a flight attendant. And I have acquired skills, abilities and experiences that will be of value in this work." List examples of each.

- Inability to describe personal characteristics, skills and goals as they relate to the job. Take time beforehand to examine your strengths, weaknesses, what you have to offer, and why you will be a valuable employee.

- Negative comments about past employers, co-workers or supervisors. Be positive when sharing information about present and past employers. If you cannot be positive, say nothing to indicate that you were hassled, that you found others difficult or annoying, or that you developed pet peeves on the job.

- Indications of a weak work ethic and poor performance standards. If you have indicated that you may get poor references because of past attitude, attendance or undependability, you had better be well prepared to give a detailed and exonerating explanation.

- Giving more emphasis to what the company can do for you than to what you can do for the company. Always, your emphasis must be on yourself as an asset to the airline.

- Knowing nothing about the job description. The lifestyle of a flight attendant calls for a person who is willing to work any day of the week, any hour of the day, holidays included. It requires a personable, sociable, patient, sensitive and caring, responsible, proactive personality. It demands some sacrifice. Be sure you know how flexible a lifestyle is required of you and how great the demands will be before you even show up for an interview. You must give the impression of being able to offer all of these qualities and concessions — without hesitation or regret! You must appear to regard hardship as high adventure and a great calling.

- Knowing nothing about the company or the airline industry. Do your homework on the airline with which you are interviewing and know plenty about the industry of which it is part. Minimal knowledge: where the flight attendant bases are, some of the aircraft in the company's fleet, and the route structure over which the airline operates. By far the vast majority of airline employees are highly loyal and dedicated to their company. Knowing some of the company history, who the company president is, the standing of the company in the industry and other company-related matters will impress your interviewers favorably.

- Relocation problems. Nine times out of ten, relocation is a part of the job as a new flight attendant. Inability or unwillingness or even hesitancy to relocate could knock you out of the competition.

- Uncertainty about when you can start training. Be specific if asked when you can start. Your interviewer is asking because the company needs to know. Do not hesitate to say that you must give your present employer a two-week notice. The airline will expect the same courtesy from you if you plan to leave it and will respect the consideration you are showing to those who currently write your paycheck. If you are available immediately, this fact could give the airline an opportunity to use you sooner.

A word of caution: An offer of training usually is valid for three to six months, depending on the carrier's policy. If you are unavailable until some time afterward, you most likely will have to begin the hiring process all over. If you have an availability problem, you perhaps should wait until that is cleared up before you start the interview process. In any event, check with the airline beforehand to make sure you are not spinning your wheels.

If you are able to respond in a calm, relaxed, prepared way to questions pertaining to the issues listed above, you will have the edge on your competition for the job. Your responses (formulated, at least in part, beforehand) should incorporate the "good flight attendant" qualities on which you will be evaluated during the interview.

Interviewing, after all, is a question-and-answer session to determine whether or not a candidate has the attitude and abilities that have been determined to be key qualities in the best job performance.

Keep that in mind. It will help you through the stress questions of your interview. It can make you a star performer.

and one facial portrait are the usual requirements. The photos should be of you alone, looking your best.

Having a list of references along will help show that you are organized. If you have letters of recommendation that you would like to submit, have copies on hand; never submit any original paperwork since it may not be returned.

The prospective employer will want your Social Security number. If you are not a U.S. citizen, you will be asked for your work card or green card. By law, you cannot be hired without one.

A doctor's verification of your physical status may be necessary in some cases. For instance, if your vision could be a concern because it is at the edge of acceptable limits, you may be well advised to have an eye exam and bring the results along to your interview. If you wear braces but your orthodontist has indicated that they will come off soon, bring verification of this fact with you. Being a step ahead of potential detours could avoid a delay of several weeks in your acceptance for training.

If the weather is not cooperating on the day of your interview and a coat or umbrella is needed, decorum should be observed. An umbrella should be of the collapsing type. Shake it out and fold it up, if possible, before entering the building. In any event, avoid creating a mess with it in the waiting area. If you are wearing a raincoat, take it off after you check in with the receptionist and ask where you might hang it. There is usually a coat rack or other provision for rain wear.

Be on your good behavior with this receptionist. The receptionist counts more than you might think.

The Waiting Room

Your first contact in the reception area will be with the secretary or receptionist. The receptionist is the hotline to the office staff. If she observes what appears to be inappropriate behavior in the waiting area, she will report it. If you are abrasive, overly aggressive, or rude, the office staff will know this before you ever meet them. No matter how qualified or well-prepared you are, your chances could be doomed in the waiting area if you act like a jerk. (Note well: The interviewer is not a passive recipient of bad tidings; sometimes the interviewer asks the receptionist for an impression of you.)

If you have been invited to fly to another city for your interview, the need to mind your P's and Q's begins at the airport. If the ticket agent, flight attendant or any other employee finds your behavior offensive, the unfavorable impression will be reported either verbally or in writing. Current employees of the airline want to work with people who will behave professionally at all times; they feel duty-bound to report potential problems.

There even have been occasions when hotel personnel have reported interviewees who have created problems while overnighting. Never forget that you are interviewing to become an airline professional; your professionalism should shine through even in the midst of unforeseen travel glitches or inattentive hotel service.

From the moment you step into the building where the interview is being held, do not smoke or chew gum — even if you are invited to do so. Chewing gum is downright rude. Some people feel that they can hide gum in their mouths while they use it as a breath freshener. They are wrong; airline interviewers look for gum chewing because gum in your mouth while in uniform on the job is strictly prohibited. As for smoking, you are taking a serious and unnecessary chance if you smoke during a break or at any other time. This habit is a real turnoff to some people; your interviewer could be one of them. If you are a compulsive chain smoker, you cannot handle the job of flight attendant anyway because some airlines prohibit smoking outright on company premises, and all forbid you to light up while actively performing flight attendant duties (although a flight attendant can smoke while on break).

One final suggestion for the last hour before your interview: When in a stressful situation, some of us feel our throats close up; tight vocal chords are the culprit. Public speakers often sing out loud or talk to themselves to warm up their throats on the way to an engagement. The same device may help you, too.

Meeting the Interviewer

The previous chapter told you the basic dos and don'ts of meeting the interviewer, but to review:

Employment decisions can be made on the first impression, which occurs in a fleeting moment. By the time you sit down in the interviewer's office, the moment that you should have seized can have fled, and the interviewer can have formed an enduring negative impression.

Is this fair? No. But life is like this; you make the same quick judgments yourself.

In *Airline Pilot Interviews*, Irv Jasinski writes (for pilots, but relevantly for anyone seeking a job):

> . . . When the interviewer approaches you and introduces himself or herself, rise in a brisk but smooth manner, look straight into his or her eyes, smile, present a firm handshake,

and say, "It's a pleasure to meet you, Captain/Mr./Ms./Mrs./Miss. . . !" (When you don't smile, you may appear to be unfriendly, tense, uptight, or frightened.) The interviewer should never have to stand with his or her hand out, waiting for you to get up and shake hands. If the interviewer does not introduce himself or herself and remains silent to see what you will do in such a situation, it is then acceptable to introduce yourself. This can display tactful initiative on your part, under stress. . . .

When you accompany the interviewer to the interviewing office, never drop behind more than half a step, making it difficult for him or her to carry on a brief conversation with you while walking. The interviewer should not have to slow down for you.

As noted previously, wait until the interviewer invites you to sit before doing so. If there is no invitation, sit down in unison with the interviewer, or seconds later. If you are facing a panel, sit down as the last panel member sits down.

Put your purse or briefcase on the floor next to you and keep your hands folded in your lap but not clenched. Do not cross your legs unless the interviewer cannot see them. Relax and feel confident; after all, you have prepared well, and the interviewer would like to think well of you.

Always address the interviewer by Mr., Mrs., or Ms. even if this individual seems very relaxed and open. By using the first name, you may come across as too presumptuous and familiar.

During your interview, the interviewer's telephone calls should be on hold. However, should a call come in, offer to leave the room until the telephone call is over. If motioned to stay, try to act uninterested in the call.

Since some interviewers are amateurs at the business of interviewing, you may have to stay alert to the necessity of keeping the conversation on track and rolling along. Stay focused on why you are there: to sell yourself.

Do not seem overly anxious about salary and benefits. It is easy to get a published salary guide without having to ask the interviewer about pay. Since the benefits may not be published, you may be on safe ground to ask about travel passes and insurance, but you should remember that your purpose is to show the company what you can do for them; they already know that they have a lot to offer you.

Keep in mind that you are being judged constantly during your interview on a variety of characteristics. Poise, good manners self-esteem and confidence in your ability will be among your critical success factors. Your critical success factors are those aspects of the image that you are projecting which will go farthest toward getting you hired.

Do not try to prolong the interview once it obviously is over. When the interviewer has run out of questions and you have run out of information to impart, the interview is finished. Do not start small talk at this point or begin trying to bring out minor details of your dossier or of your qualifications for flight attending. By now, the interviewer already has made up his or her mind, perhaps in your favor. Do not blow it!

If you have not explicitly been offered the job, you may ask which way you will be notified (by phone or by mail), or whether it will be all right for you to call back in a few days to learn the company's decision. After this there is nothing more you can do that will have a positive impact on your chances, so simply thank the interviewer for his or her time, express again how much this job means to you, and leave.

Remember to say "Thank you" to the receptionist.

Follow-Up

After each interview write a short thank-you note to your interviewer expressing your appreciation for his or her time and helpfulness. State again that you are very enthusiastic about this job and that you hope to hear from the company soon. Mail the note immediately, before your interviewer has a chance to forget you. This promptly mailed note, which is nothing short of minimal good manners, can be the distinguishing factor between two applicants of equal ability.

Enter all interview details in your interview log. Include the name of the interviewer, the firm, and your overall immpressions and comments. This may be the last log entry you have to make, but you cannot know this until you get the call or other notification to report to training.

If you fail to land this job, be positive about the experience and knowledge you have gained for future flight attendant interviews.

CHAPTER 11

Really Following Up

There are two possibilities in the mail: You got your chance; you did not get it.

Let's say the news comes, and it is sweet. You have been invited to training. If this is the job for which you were searching, your quest is over. You have only to apply yourself and do the best that you possibly can, and the odds are very much in your favor that you will complete training successfully and be assigned a domicile. The only following up that you have ahead of you is the career track kind: pursuing your responsibilities with all the vigor and effort that is in you.

If the job you have landed is not with a major airline and is to you only a step on the way to your career goal (a position with a major carrier), then your quest is not over, and you have a more complex kind of following up to do. The balancing act for you psychologically is to maintain dual goals. For now, you have the same duty laid upon you as if you were being hired for your dream job: pursuing your responsibilities with all the vigor and effort that is in you. The hard part for you will be reminding yourself that your career goal can be attained only by just such wholehearted commitment. If your loyalty or responsibility flags, you will sabotage your long-range ambition.

More on this topic in a later chapter. For now, our focus is again the mail. Let's say the news comes and is bad: no training for you, not at this time.

The sting of disappointment takes lots of forms. Anger is one; self-doubt is a second form; bitterness a third.

If a good cry helps you get these emotions out of your system, then have a hearty cry. If a titanic fit of paranoid rage will purge you, then have at it; rage away, as long as you refrain from any foolish action.

By whatever means — a trip to the beach, a night on the town, a chess tournament — whatever turns you on and your disappointment off — get rid of the negative emotions kicked up by that envelope in the mail.

Once rejected, you are rejected — maybe for all time. Perhaps you made an irremediably bad impression on someone at this particular airline. Whatever the reason, do not dwell on a "defeat."

Call it a "setback," roll up your sleeves, and start planning and analyzing for your next attack.

Really, your follow-up is your not accepting a rejection as a defeat. Defeated people quit; they surrender. Be one of the unvanquished. Be more than a survivor; be a conqueror.

Some people are rebuffed once and throw in the towel. Others are knocked down time and again and keep coming back until they win.

You know which type you want to be.

After each interview is over, put on your thinking cap. Evaluate your responses and reactions during the interview process. Do not put yourself down; nonetheless, what's done is done, and rationalization of your performance to make it seem better in your own mind than it really was is fruitless and counterproductive. It is counterproductive because it will keep you from making adjustments in your performance the next time you are called for an interview.

Be objective. Go over in your mind the qualities that were evaluated — the qualities that somebody important decided you did not have in sufficient development to be invited for training.

The Criteria of Self-Evaluation

- Attitude. Were your responses positive or negative? Were you able to turn some negatives into positives?

- Courtesy/friendliness. How did you react to everyone involved with your interview? Were you friendly to the recruiter? Did you establish good eye contact? If there were others interviewing with you, were you friendly and successful at helping them feel at ease? Did you know that you were expected to help others feel at ease? Were there moments during the interview process when you may have withdrawn into yourself a bit, just long enough for somebody to notice? Did you know that such behavior might be regarded as a sign of insufficient energy and sociability for the job? If you checked in with a secretary, were you courteous and smiling, and did you give her correct information without any sign of wanting to hold back or question her right to ask for it? Were there moments when you perhaps allowed signs of criticism or of cynicism to show in your face? Were you, in fact, courteous and friendly at all times?

- Dependability. During the course of the interview, did you convey how dependable you are, explaining any apparent deficiencies in your past job performance? (A bit of honesty here might help: Is your record defensible? If not, you may have to postpone your flight attending ambitions for a while until you have established a track record showing that you have matured.)

- Enthusiasm. Were you prepared and excited about the potential of being employed by this company, or were you too nervous to let your enthusiasm shine through? Did you convey that you feel good about yourself and your accomplishments?

- Honesty. Were you realistic about your track record? Or did you attempt to cover up some areas that really required an explanation?

- Initiative. Were you able to relate some instances of initiative on your part in work, school or community activities? During the interview process, did your actions demonstrate initiative without trespassing into pushiness?

- Loyalty. If you are loyal to your employers but your application reads as if you were a "job hopper," did you take the time to explain, or did you leave the situation up to the recruiter's imagination?

- Morality. Is there anything in your past that would indicate that you do not have high moral standards? Can it be explained? Is there some other strategy, short of an attempted cover-up, that would more effectively combat the suggestion of the incident, whatever it was? Did you do everything possible during the interview process to make people want to revise the impression created by the past incident?

- Maturity. Did you conduct yourself in a poised, professional manner? Does your record support your effort to portray yourself as mature?

- Punctuality. As noted earlier, any tardiness at all can disqualify you with some airlines. If you walked into the reception area breathless at 30 seconds past time for your interview to begin, you may have to look no further for the cause of your rejection.

- Self-control. Were you composed throughout the interview process? No momentary panic? Were you conservative in behavior and ideas? Did you react quickly and decisively to situations?

- Sense of humor. Laughing breaks the ice. It takes the edge off everyone's tension. Were you too serious, too dour, too ill at ease with the recruiter and others?

- Tact. Failures of tact come off as rudeness. Were you sensitive to others' feelings, thoughtful of their needs?

- Voice tone. Is your habitual tone pleasant? At the interviews, did your voice convey warmth, interest and a contact personality? Or were you so nervous that your voice was wooden and flat? Do you need to work on voice modulation? Did you use reasonably good grammar and pronunciation? Mangling these too much can ruin the effect of even the most mellifluous voice.

Airlines' reasons for not hiring applicants fall roughly under the heads of personal presentation, personal attributes, prior employment and education, and apparent motivation. At the risk of some repetitions of previous points, specific causes for rejection include:

Personal presentation:

- Poor personal appearance.

- "Superiority complex," or know-it-all, aggressive, overbearing attitude.

- Poor communication skills, including problems with voice, diction or grammar, or inability to say what you want to say.

- Lack of confidence and poise; appearance of being nervous, ill at ease, or unfocused.

- Failure to participate in activities and conversation.

- Evasiveness in answering questions.

- Lack of tact and sensitivity to others.

- Lack of courtesy and consistent good will shown to others.

- Poor eye contact with the interviewer.

- Rambling responses; responses that make no point.

- Sloppy application.

- Very little sense of humor.

- Bringing friends or family to the interview.

- Overemphasis on whom the applicant knows.

- Arriving late.

- Failure to express verbal appreciation for the interviewer's time.

Personal attributes:

- Lack of interest and enthusiasm.

- Lack of maturity.

- Lack of energy and vitality.

- Indecisiveness.

- Friction with parents, peers, employers.

- Lack of flexibility with regard to work schedule and domicile.

- Cynicism about the job and the airline.
- Low moral standards.
- Radical ideas.
- Narrow interests.
- High-pressure personality.
- Lazy attitude.
- Poor handling of personal finances.
- Inability to take constructive criticism.

Prior employment/education:

- Poor overall scholastic record.
- Condemnation of past teachers/employers.
- Marked dislike for previous work.
- Lack of job-related experiences.
- Instability of work record.
- Poor attendance record.
- Poor recommendations from previous employers.

Motivation:

- Lack of purpose and/or goals.
- Overemphasis on money and benefits; on what the company can do for the applicant rather than on what the applicant can contribute to the job.
- Lack of real interest in flight attending.
- Looking for a foot in the door; job shopping.

- Desiring the job because it leaves time to pursue other goals; desiring the job short-term.

- Lack of familiarity with the company.

- "Just heard you were hiring."

What Purpose Self-Knowledge?

Having completed your self-evaluation, is there any good thing that you can do with it?

Sure there is. You can use it to present a better image at your next interview session.

There are numerous flight attendants who tell of returning to the same company two or three times before being offered a position. They were rejected once, twice; but they were persistent, and they got their jobs.

You may simply need to put more effort into your presentation. Interviewing is a learned skill. As with any other skill, practice makes perfect — or, at least, much better.

Again, interviewing involves so many variables (e.g., your state of mind, your confidence level, your rapport with the person interviewing you) that intangibles could have caused your setback. The same intangibles may not be present next time you interview.

Do not waste a moment on regrets. Get busy planning the next attack, either at the same airline (which, after all, may not have closed the door to you permanently) or at some other carrier.

With persistence, you will succeed unless, after all, flight attending was not meant to be the career for you.

The truth, however, is that you can tell whether or not you are cut out to be a flight attendant. All you have to do is make an honest evaluation of yourself in the light of the demands made on flight attendants. And if you are right for the role, you will get to play it.

But you do have to follow up — really follow up. No faint hearts need apply.

Part III

BEGINNING YOUR CAREER

CHAPTER 12

Your Training

Everything you have learned about the flight attendant role and image comes into play during training. Your airline wants you to help market its product by projecting an attractive, thoroughly professional image. It wants your standards of conduct and of work performance to carry through with the image.

Your airline needs efficient, safe work habits in all of its flight attendants. It desires that you be well-versed in emergency procedures and that you demonstrate the presence of mind to handle an emergency. You should be familiar enough with the aircraft and with other aspects of flight that you recognize immediately when a potentially hazardous situation is presenting itself.

Your airline wants you to be positive; mature; personable but firm; conscientious in performing duties; punctual and reliable; and knowledgeable in all aspects of your job.

That is, it wants an excellent flight attendant.

An Overview of Training

Training varies from airline to airline, but it usually lasts from two to six weeks. In most cases, it is paid for by the airline, although there are a few carriers that charge for training and/or trainee accommodations. In these cases, payroll deduction is available after a down payment has been made.

Training takes place in designated classroom facilities, usually at a primary base location. Trainees stay in a nearby hotel. Generally, lodging is paid for by the company, but meals are not. Most airlines pay for daily expenses at their normal per diem rates.

The training is costly for the airline or expensive for you, as the case may be; comprehensive; and very demanding. You must maintain a predetermined grade point average (the exact grade depends on the airline) and a high standard of conduct throughout your training. You will be weighed periodically during training to make sure that your weight is not fluctuating.

The schooling covers four broad areas: safety and first aid; service to passengers; appearance and image; and operational protocol.

Safety embraces hazard prevention, response to emergency situations, and first aid/CPR (cardio-pulmonary resuscitation). Broadly, it also includes such aspects of security as how to deal with bomb threats, highjackings, and terrorists.

Operational protocol embraces two main areas: flight responsibilities and company familiarization. Flight responsibilities include aircraft familiarization, inside and outside; flight attendant contract provisions and work rules; personal and passenger safety; and general flight attendant responsibilities before, during, and after each flight. Company familiarization includes an introduction to the company; flight attendant standards of performance and conduct; training sessions; and supervisory meetings. It may also include a flight attendant union presentation.

The other two study areas are what they sound like; again, however, specific content varies widely from airline to airline. Broadly, service includes both customer interaction skills and food and beverage procedures and techniques. Appearance and image includes grooming, uniform and appearance standards, and comportment while interacting with customers.

Some airlines also give instruction in wellness.

While training categories are separate, in practice they are integrated. For example, service is affected by the specific aircraft on which you will be working. A very obvious situation is the small commuter airplane that just cannot accommodate meal service, not only because the cabin is too close for such activities but also because a situation that regional airlines often refer to as "the fanny factor" comes into play: Flights of more than an hour and 10 minutes on these small aircraft can become extremely uncomfortable for passengers, so the carrier does not schedule longer flights in them. An hour or so is insufficient time in which to handle a meal service (a considerable part of that time is consumed by takeoff, climb, descent, and landing).

A less obvious example is wide-body versus narrow-body meal service. In a narrow cabin with only a single narrow aisle, maneuverability of the service carts becomes an issue. The carts are heavy and hard to handle. It can take quite a long time to maneuver the equipment from one end of the cabin to the other. Thus, service often cannot be quite as elaborate on such aircraft as on those with two aisles. The service also will not entail an extra deck of passengers or using a dumbwaiter or the stairs to reach that upper deck with food and drink items. Again, the routes flown affect the type of service. The routes flown by the big wide-body jets tend to be longer than those flown by small narrow-bodies; longer routes permit more elaborate service. Finally, wide-bodies contain a "lower-lobe galley," i.e., kitchen facilities one story below the main passenger cabin, and this large kitchen can make more elaborate service possible — or it can make your job a lot harder, depending on the aircraft and its equippage and configuration.

Usually included in the operational protocol is schooling in provisions of the contract under which the particular carrier's flight attendants work. Trainees also are taught scheduling procedures and other aspects of company operations and rules, including how to wear the uniform and how to vary the uniform from day to day. Your grooming and personal appearance will be checked for conformity with company standards on a daily basis during training.

Trainees are familiarized with the equipment on every type of aircraft in the airline's fleet. This part of the training has a special bearing on safety, including emergency procedures. Flight attendants learn the correct evacuation procedures for each type of aircraft flown. The equipment is different from airplane to airplane.

At larger carriers, you will be taught evacuation techniques in aircraft simulators that reproduce the conditions of an airplane in distress, replete with lurching and tilting of the aircraft, simulated fire, smoke in the cabin, and screaming voices. At smaller airlines, training is less elaborate, but you still must learn how to evacuate the carrier's aircraft in 90 seconds or less, in order to conform with Federal Aviation Administration (FAA) safety standards.

The emergency scenario walk-through, which has to be undergone by flight attendants, involves a simulated accident with "loud noises as if the aircraft has come to an abrupt stop, hit something," according to Nancy Gilmer, coordinator of air safety and health research for the Association of Flight Attendants. "Then you have so many seconds to perform certain duties — notify the cockpit, shout a set of commands to passengers, look for indications of fire — usually there will be smoke — decide which exit is the safest, and actually go down the chute."

FA RESPONSIBILITIES: WORDS ARE SUITED TO ACTIONS AND SETTING

A flight attendant's responsibilities in an emergency landing and evacuation include specific commands. These commands vary according to the aircraft in which the flight is taking place. Following are the flight attendant commands for an emergency descent and evacuation over land, as given in one airline's in-flight manual.

FLIGHT ATTENDANT COMMANDS

A. Unplanned/Planned Emergency
   (1) Flight Attendant Brace Command: "BEND OVER HEADS DOWN"
   (2) Initiating Evacuation Commands:
      (a) "UNFASTEN SEAT BELTS AND GET OUT"
      (b) "LEAVE EVERYTHING"
      (c) "HOLD THOSE PEOPLE BACK"
   (3) (727/737/MD-80/DC-9) Doors with Slides:
      (a) "COME THIS WAY"
      (b) "SLIDE, SLIDE, SLIDE"
      (c) "RUN AWAY FROM THE PLANE"
   (4) (727/737-100) Doors with Stairs:
      (a) "COME THIS WAY"
      (b) "RUN DOWN THE STAIRS AND AWAY FROM THE PLANE"
   (5) (727/737/MD-80/DC-9) Window Exits:
      (a) "COME THIS WAY"

These evacuation procedures, including the shouted commands, are mandated by the FAA, and you must have the FAA manual open while giving instructions to passengers. You can be fined by the FAA if you do not have your up-to-date manual accessible at all times on a flight. The emergency commands are different for various aircraft, e.g., doors on the McDonnell-Douglas Super 80 are not the same as those on a Boeing 747, and procedures thus are different.

There is also overwater training for those flight attendants who may be working flights that will be routed more than 50 miles from the mainland. This training involves a combination of classroom work and practice in "ditching" and in how to deploy the life rafts and survive on the high seas. Actually being in the water in a training session can be a gripping experience.

Every year, by law, a flight attendant has to undergo recurrent classroom training in emergency procedures. The actual "walk-through" of these proce-

(b) "STEP THROUGH — FOOT FIRST"
(c) "SLIDE OFF THE BACK OF THE WING"
(d) "RUN AWAY FROM THE PLANE"
(6) (747/DC-10/A-300) All Doors Except 3L/R:
(a) "COME THIS WAY"
(b) "FORM TWO LINES"
(c) "JUMP AND SLIDE"
(d) "RUN AWAY FROM THE PLANE"
(7) (727/DC-10) At Doors 3L and 3R:
(a) "COME THIS WAY"
(b) "FORM TWO LINES"
(c) "RUN JUMP INTO THE SLIDE"
(d) "RUN AWAY FROM THE PLANE"
(8) (A-300) At Doors 3L and 3R:
(a) "COME THIS WAY"
(b) "JUMP AND SLIDE"
(c) "RUN AWAY FROM THE PLANE"
(9) 747 Crew Service Door:
(a) "COME THIS WAY"
(b) "FORM ONE LINE"
(c) "SLIDE, SLIDE, SLIDE"
(d) "RUN AWAY FROM THE PLANE"
(10) Redirection Techniques:
(a) "THIS EXIT BLOCKED"
(b) "TURN AROUND"
(c) "GO THAT WAY"

dures has to be accomplished not only in initial training, but every two years in recurrent training.

To a very large extent, the flight attendant's job — and therefore flight attendant training — is governed by FAA rules. You will learn these rules in order to enforce them at boarding and takeoff, en route, and during and immediately after landing.

(If you would like to look them over now, Appendix A contains most of the FAA regulations applying to flight attending, either directly or indirectly.)

Part of your schooling will consist of hands-on training and observation/training flights. The FAA requirement is that a new flight attendant put in at least five hours working a flight under training supervision, but this requirement can be waived down to $2^{1}/_{2}$ hours at the airline's request if the airline can show the FAA that the training achieved in $2^{1}/_{2}$ hours is adequate.

Throughout your training, you should apply yourself totally. There is nothing to hold back for; you are getting the chance for a great career. Do not be intimidated by the training. It is tough, but fewer than one percent of trainees fail to complete the course.

A Flight Attendant's Story

A flight attendant at a major carrier had this to say about her initial training experience:

"[Our airline training program] put a lot of emphasis on books, on how you looked, on emergency procedures.

"They wanted us to know everything by the book. They had FAA things that we had to go by; they spent a lot of time on emergency equipment and procedures. In an emergency, we have certain things that we have to say — a whole list of things that we are absolutely supposed to go by. No. 1 is most important, No. 2 next; if we only get to No. 3, that's just the way it is. We are supposed to have our manuals with us and pull them out. We can be fined by the FAA if we don't have the manual accessible. I keep my manual as close as I can to my jumpseat."

She said the trainees practiced ditching and emergency landings, including different procedures for a variety of scenarios and aircraft. For example, on a "gear up" emergency landing, which will occur when systems fail and a landing gear will not go down, flight attendants may have to take measures that are not necessary when the landing gears are working properly. If no landing gear will work, procedures will not necessarily change, but if one gear works and another does not, then the attitude of the aircraft on impact with the landing strip will be affected and so will the emergency exits that can be reached safely. Therefore, flight attendants have to move passengers to seats near those exits that probably can be most easily reached once the plane lands.

The flight attendant continued: "I felt [our instruction] was very thorough. You practiced everything. They divide you into groups of four or five, and they call your group in and one by one you go through the emergency procedures. Then they talk about things you did or said wrong, or maybe left out.

"We did not get CPR-certified. We were trained to do mouth-to-mouth resuscitation. It is CPR, but we are never actually certified. I had been certified before when I worked for a medical clinic, so it was pretty easy for me. I felt they were pretty thorough under the circumstances. They're hiring people with all sorts of backgrounds — you no longer have to be a nurse to be a flight attendant.

"As far as how you looked, they would put lists on the board — meaning, for example, that not everyone had on enough lipstick. We also had to go for a makeup evaluation. They took a look at our makeup to see what we were wearing; they would OK some items and reject others. We were weighed once a week.

". . . We were pretty much under the microscope.

"We had mockups of the inside of an airplane. We used that not only for practicing emergency drills but for getting used to what it's like working inside a cabin. . . . Out of six weeks, we probably spent four or five days actually working on the service end of our job. You practice serving drinks, for example. Basically, the food and beverage training is getting used to working with the carts."

The flight attendant, who did not wish to be identified, said trainees had to learn what was inside the first-aid kit; however, FAA rules mandate that only a certified medical doctor or registered nurse use the kit, and there are forms that the flight attendant and doctor or nurse must fill out when a medical emergency arises.

The core aspect of training was the degree to which a trainee had to master professionalism as a service representative and safety expert, conforming to and always reflecting the company image, she said.

Example of a Major Program

A training manual will lay out each step of the program, along with the objectives of each session, what will be covered in each session, what you will be expected to know or be able to do as a result of the session, and how you will be tested.

To complete the program successfully, you must meet both the academic standards for tests and the airline's "training performance standards."

One major airline divides the training performance standards into four broad categories: manner; job knowledge/skills; appearance; and dependability. The overall objective of each of these categories is as follows:

- Manner. Demonstrate good judgment, mature behavior, and a positive attitude toward the job and others.

- Job knowledge/skills. Demonstrate the ability to learn and perform the duties of a flight attendant.

- Appearance. Consistently meet flight attendant appearance standards and grooming objectives required in training.

- Dependability. Demonstrate that you can be counted on to meet obligations in a responsible fashion with a minimum of direction/follow-up by superiors or fellow flight attendants.

The thoroughness of this airline's evaluation is illustrated by a breakdown of the qualities evaluated in just one of the categories, that of manner. Manner includes:

- Presents a favorable image of [the airline].

- Projects warmth and openness.

- Confronts and solves problems in a positive way.

- Displays consideration of others.

- Demonstrates patience and self-control.

- Is receptive to suggestions for self improvement.

- Shows an interest in learning and performing the flight attendant job.

- Demonstrates an interest in the opinions of others.

- Is cooperative in working with others.

- Has a positive sense of humor.

- Is able to tolerate frustration and maintain flexibility when under pressure.

- Demonstrates a concern for total customer service.

When you report for training, you must already have familiarized yourself with the 24-hour clock and the routes, stations, geography and time zones of the airline. During training, you will be tested on all of these topics. The program utilizes Learning Resource Centers (LRCs), computerized training cubicles that offer an array of self-teach video modules. LRC modules include such topics as aircraft familiarization, a current-issues program, new procedures and technology, safety, service procedures, a language series (for international domiciles only), and two "key position" modules, one for domestic flights, the other for international. A "key position" is either chief purser, aft purser, or another senior flight attendant with critical responsibilities (say, the flight attendant in charge of the upper deck on a Boeing 747).

During your first week, you will learn to use remote computer terminals (CRTs) to access basic flight attendant information. As is typical at all airlines, you will be taught to read timetables, tickets and the OAG (Official Airline Guide).

Instructional methods include lectures, practical application or hands-on experience onboard the aircraft and on training flights, self-instructional workbooks, self-quizzes, group discussion, written and practical tests, and interactive workshops.

Base assignments are awarded at graduation, and you start probation. A new life is beginning for you, including, probably, a new and perhaps exciting place of residence.

CHAPTER 13

The Workplace

The aircraft that serve as the "office" for a flight attendant's work day are true chariots of fire: They are driven by either turboprop or turbofan engines, both of which depend for propulsive power on the energy generated by intense heat and compression.

These aircraft are a great deal faster and safer than the piston-powered airplanes that preceded them because turbine engines are more powerful than piston engines and stand up better to the rugged demands of high-cycle flying. They have made the flight attendant's job less glamorous, perhaps, than in years past, but safer and more rewarding. They have revolutionized the airline industry and the way people travel; thus, they also have helped reshape the business and social environment.

In the sailing ship era, a transatlantic journey took months. The advent of engine-powered oceanliners cut the journey to weeks. Now the same trip takes a day by jet.

No one should be surprised that such a technological galaxy has become an international one: One of the most popular regional airliners is made in Brazil, another very popular one is produced in Sweden, and a third is a French-Italian product; a consortium of companies in five European countries manufactures the Airbus, which competes with Boeing, McDonnell-Douglas and Lockheed aircraft for the dollars spent by U.S. airlines on their jet fleets; the Fokker F-28 and Fokker 100 are Dutch jetliners; the BAe 146 passenger jet is made by British Aerospace; and the Concorde is a French-British product.

Of the aircraft mentioned above, the Concorde, because of its supersonic speed and high noise levels, is the best-known, but it has had the least impact on U.S. airlines and upon the world of flight attendants. The Airbus 300 series and the two Fokker jets are flown by several major and national airlines in the United States. In the 1980s the BAe 146 became the first step up to jetliners for a number of emergent national-size carriers (airlines with more than $100,000 in annual revenue). The Embraer Brasilia, the Saab 340 and the Aerospatiale-Aeritalia ATR 42 are being flown by a combined total of close to 20 regional airlines that feed passengers to such majors as United, American, TWA, Northwest, Delta, Continental and USAir.

Other European nations involved in the manufacture of commuter aircraft are West Germany, Spain and Ireland. Short Brothers of Ireland, now owned by Bombardier, the parent company of Canadair, has had considerable success with its unpressurized turboprop aircraft at U.S. commuter/regional airlines. Indonesia has joined with Spain to produce a utility turboprop.

Boeing and McDonnell-Douglas continue to have the most jet aircraft in world airline fleets, and Lockheed is a third U.S. competitor. Two U.S. companies, Fairchild and Beech, produce 19-passenger aircraft for commuter/regional airline use, and a Canadian manufacturer, de Havilland, is now owned by Boeing. Boeing/de Havilland is the producer of two turboprop aircraft that are in wide use at commuter/regional airlines, in North America and in the rest of the world.

The foregoing summary does not count military and corporate aircraft or the several dozen countries that are involved in manufacture of either airframe parts (ailerons, wings, radomes, etc.) or airplane components (engines, landing gears, propellers, fuel pumps, avionics, etc.).

The disparate origins of aircraft and their components, as well as the variety of aircraft types, have an impact on the flight attendant's job. Doors are different from aircraft to aircraft. So are seating arrangements, foot and leg room, baggage room, and seat pitch (the maximum angle to which seats can be moved for greatest relaxation). Emergency exits are not the same from plane to plane. Some airplanes have more noise or greater vibration than others. Often, flight attendants at regional airlines find themselves needing to reassure passengers about the quality of a foreign-built aircraft, especially those older-generation turboprop airplanes with relatively high levels of cabin noise and vibration.

The flight attendant's job will be different from one type of airplane to another, depending on how many flight attendants are required on the type, what the configuration of the aircraft is, how new the plane is, how much it has been modernized if it is an older model, and so on. The broad divisions of aircraft on which flight attendants work are as follows.

Heavy Jet: By definition, a heavy jet is any aircraft weighing 300,000 pounds or more, gross weight. Examples of aircraft in this category are the DC-8, DC-10, B-767, B-747, L-1011 and A-300.

Large Transport Aircraft: Any aircraft weighing 12,500 to 299,999 pounds, gross weight. Examples are the B-727, B-737 and DC-9 at the upper end, and the ATR 42, Saab 340 and Brasilia near the lower end.

Configuration of aircraft plays a large role in how easy or difficult a flight attendant's job can be. There is a vast difference between working in an all-coach configuration of a Boeing 727 and a full-service configuration of the same airplane. In an all-coach 727, the airline puts extra seats where a galley would have been, or it combines a number of extra seats with a very abbreviated galley. There will be one less restroom on the all-coach plane. The space in the aisles will not change, but because the bulkheads are removed, everything is a lot tighter. Passengers lose leg room because the space between the rows of seats is reduced.

Such a configuration is used on flights that do not require meal catering, as on business shuttle flights between New York and Boston. Occasionally such aircraft wind up in an airline's wider system for a few days, and then flight attendants must cope with some real problems. Said one flight attendant: "All-coach shuttle airplanes in the Northeast corridor are not set up for full-service flights. There is no room for trash, no room for storage of service items, so you just have to come up with your own system."

Getting stuck with such an aircraft on a full-service flight means that the flight attendants must serve a cold snack and find ways to cope with other problems that arise, such as the numerous seat-number problems. "All-coach changes the seating configuration in terms of the way the seats and rows are numbered, so if someone purchases a seat two months in advance, this can make for huge problems for the flight attendants. There are all kinds of seat duplications, and someone who thought he had a first-class seat would find no first-class on the plane," she explained.

Crew complement can make a big difference, too. On a DC-9, for example, the minimum flight attendant crew is two. If the other flight attendant happens to be someone who does not work as hard as you do, you could be in for a difficult trip.

Galley systems are important as well. Newer aircraft types, such as the Boeing 757 and 767, have a much easier galley system to work with than do the older types. The system on the new airplanes includes carts that are pre-loaded with food. Flight attendants take the carts up and down the aisles, as opposed to having to run up and down the aisles hand-carrying food from the galley to the passengers.

The Lockheed L-1011 was one of the first aircraft to have a cart system; the system was made necessary by the fact that the galley is in the belly of the plane. However, flight attendants say the original L-1011 carts are very hard to maneuver. Since reconfiguring the L-1011s with newer carts is quite expensive, there remain a good many L-1011s in service with the old cart system.

With this overview as background, here are some basic facts about specific aircraft that you may encounter as a flight attendant. Only some of the more prevalent aircraft are included in this account.

Regional/Commuter Aircraft

ATR 42 and ATR 72 The Aerospatiale-Aeritalia ATR 42 is in wide use at regional airlines in the United States; the stretch version of this aircraft, the ATR 72, has sold mainly in Europe. These two aircraft are turboprop (turbine/propeller-driven) airliners that fit well into the fleet mix of companies that own both major and regional airlines. The ATR 42 and 72 have the advantage of being large enough to inspire confidence in passengers. Texas Air Corp., parent of Continental and Eastern, and AMR Corp., parent of American, own ATR 42s that are flown by their feeder airlines.

The ATR 42 is 74.3 feet long and has a wing span of 80 feet, 7 inches. Depending on configuration, it seats from 46 to 50 passengers and cruises at around 267 knots (nautical miles per hour).* It calls for only one flight attendant. Since the average flight is only about 50 to 70 minutes in duration, the flight attendant seldom has to worry about meal service (and then only a cold snack), but peanuts and beverage service are a standard part of flight attendant duties on the ATR 42.

The ATR 72 is 89.1 feet long and has a wing span of 88 feet, 9 inches. It generally seats from 64 to 68 passengers and cruises at around 282 knots. The ATR 72 is only slightly faster than the ATR 42 and is therefore used for the same kind of flight (50 to 70 minutes). Because of its capacity, the ATR 72 calls for two flight attendants. The aircraft is large enough to keep them quite busy with beverage/peanut service and the cold snack that some regional airlines have added to a few of their flights. For flight attendants, there is a big difference between working high-density and low-density versions of the ATR 72, if for no other reason than that the galley in the high-density version is so tiny that beverage/peanut service is all that is feasible.

---

* One international nautical mile is exactly 1.852 kilometers or approximately 1.150779 survey miles. Thus, 267 knots is roughly 307 miles per hour.

BAe 146 Turbojet   The British Aerospace BAe 146 turbojet is an extremely quiet airplane that has permitted a number of expanding regional airlines to provide jet service and to grow to hefty "national airline" size. Among feeder airlines flying the two-pilot BAe 146 are Air Wisconsin, Aspen Airways and WestAir.

The BAe 146 has gone through several models, beginning with the BAe 146-100 and climbing the ladder of power and cabin size. The BAe 146-300 is 104 feet, 2 inches long and has a wing span of 86.5 feet, but with a special wingtip similar to the arrowhead wingtips on the Airbus Industrie A310; the wingtips give the wing span an effective increase "on the order of 10 to 12 feet" and add to flight stability, according to British Aerospace. The BAe 146-300 seats from 103 to 128 passengers, depending on configuration, and it cruises at about 0.7 Mach number.* Thus, the BAe-146-300 is both fast enough and large enough to require full meal service on many flights and beverage/peanut service on all legs.

The earlier BAe 146-200 is 10 feet, 6 inches shorter than the BAe 146-300, and seats from 90 to 96 passengers. The same flight attendant service is called for in this version of the BAe-146 as in the 146-300, but the work load is obviously lighter.

Brasilia, CBA-123 and EMB-145   Embraer, a Brazilian aircraft manufacturer, has won popular acceptance of its EMB-120 Brasilia turboprop and CBA-123 pusherprop. Its EMB-145 regional jet is one of the first turbojet aircraft developed especially for commuter/regional airline service.

The two-pilot-crew, 30-passenger EMB-120 Brasilia turboprop was designed to be the smallest and fastest of its class (the Brasilia fits at the bottom end of FAR Part 121 operation and at the top end of FAR Part 135 operation). Powered by two Pratt & Whitney Canada PW115 engines that drive Hamilton-Standard propellers, the Brasilia cruises at around 300 knots (or about 350 m.p.h.). It is just over 65.6 feet long and has a wing span of 64.9 feet. Among the larger U.S. operators of the Brasilia are Texas Air Corp., which bought a fleet of them for its regional (feeder) airlines; WestAir, a United Express carrier of national airline size; and ASA, a Delta Connection carrier also of national airline size.

As with other regional airliners, the Brasilia calls for a single flight attendant whose standard duties involve beverage and peanut service, but several regional airlines provide cold snacks on the Brasilia.

---

* Mach number: a number representing the ratio of the speed of an object to the speed of sound in the surrounding medium (e.g., air) through which the object is moving. The speed of sound in air is roughly 767 miles per hour (at room temperature). Thus, 0.7 Mach number is roughly 537 miles per hour.

The CBA-123 is a 19-seat new-technology aircraft employing a pusherprop propulsion system. This speedy new plane will not normally require a flight attendant because regional airlines operate under an exemption that lets them dispense with flight attendant service on all of their aircraft that seat 19 or fewer passengers. Popular regional airline 18- and 19-seaters are the Fairchild Metro series (I, II, III, etc.), the British Aerospace Jetstream 31, and the Beech 1900 series (B, C, D). Regional airlines frequently use a tape of a flight attendant's voice on these aircraft to explain safety rules to passengers. In other instances, the captain handles the safety instructions.

Embraer's EMB-145 is noteworthy as one of the first turbojet aircraft designed specifically for commuter/regional airline use. The 45-passenger jet flies a little faster than 400 knots (460 miles per hour) at cruise and has 75 percent structural commonality with the Brasilia. It is 87.7 feet in length and 73.4 feet in wing span.

De Havilland Dash 7 and Dash 8 De Havilland Canada, now a subsidiary of Boeing Aircraft, at one time had the most ubiquitous of all commuter aircraft, the 18-seat Twin Otter, but this older-generation turboprop is seldom seen at U.S. regional airlines now. However, Boeing/de Havilland maintains its presence at commuter/regional airlines with the Dash 7 STOLcraft turboprop and the Dash 8 semi STOLcraft (STOL stands for "short takeoff and landing").

The Dash 7, a four-engine aircraft that can take off and land on very short airfields, has proven to be the turboprop of choice for airlines operating in certain demanding environments, such as the rugged mountain terrain of Norway, where Wideroe Airlines plies its trade, or the ski resort areas of the Rocky Mountains, where Rocky Mountain Airways, a Continental Commuter, serves the resort trade. The Dash 7 is the only commercial airplane that can handle the London STOLport, where Brymon Airways serves a business clientele. On the other hand, ASA of Atlanta flies the Dash 7 simply because it is a durable and economical airplane.

The 50-passenger Dash 7 is unusual in having four turboprop engines mounted on high wings with lateral-control spoilers, giving it the ability to fly steep-gradient approaches and liftoffs. It cruises at 228 knots (about 262 mph). It is 80.5 feet long; its wing span is 93 feet. From a flight attendant viewpoint, it is a rugged, safe, stand-up-cabin aircraft that can fly in any kind of climate or terrain. Passengers who are not aware of the Dash 7's excellent safety record sometimes react to the cabin noise of the plane with fear, so one of a flight attendant's tasks of some significance on the Dash 7 is to notice when a passenger seems afraid and try to sooth the passenger's nerves. As with other regional airline planes, the cold snack is sometimes part of flight attendant service. More typical is beverage and peanut service.

The twin-engined, semi-STOL Dash 8 has the same high wing and T-tail with tandem rudders that are found on the Dash 7, but it has important differences, including a smaller fuselage diameter to accommodate higher speeds (over 270 knots at cruise). It comes in two models, the Dash 8-100 and Dash 8-300. The 37-seat 8-100 has a length of 73 feet and a wing span of 85 feet. The 40-seat 8-300 is 84.25 feet long and has a 90-foot wing span. The Dash 8-100 cruises at 272 knots (roughly 313 m.p.h.), the 8-300 at 286 knots (about 329 m.p.h.).

The Dash 8 yields easier flight attendant duty than the Dash 7 because it has significantly less cabin noise and looks and feels like a real airliner to passengers. Airlines flying the Dash 8 include Eastern Metro Express, Henson (a USAir subsidiary) and Horizon (an Alaska Airlines subsidiary).

Saab 340B and Saab 2000 The Saab 340 has gained the widest acceptance among U.S. airlines of any turboprop plane in its class. AMR Eagle, Bar Harbor, Comair, Metroflight, Air Midwest and Express Airlines I/Northwest Airlink are among the carriers flying either the Saab 340A or Saab 340B or both.

Powered by two turboprop engines, the 34-passenger Saab 340B, the latest and most powerful version of the 340, does about 282 knots (about 324 m.p.h.) at cruise. It is 64 feet, 8 inches long and has a wing span of 70 feet, 4 inches. The Saab 340B gives a quiet, smooth flight that makes a flight attendant's job easy. As with other regional airliners, flight attendant duties on the Saab 340A and B include beverage/peanut service and an occasional cold snack.

The Saab 2000 had won acceptance by AMR Eagle and Northwest Airlink (Express Airlines I) even before it was completely developed. This 50-passenger, high-speed (365-knot cruise, or 425 m.p.h.) turboprop airplane is 88 feet, 8 inches long and has a wing span of 81 feet, 2 inches. It is powered by two turboprop engines driving propellers that are electrically controlled by a system integrated with the engine FADEC (Full Authority Digital Engine Control) mechanism.

Designed to compete with jet aircraft, it has avionics of equal sophistication with those of the large aircraft flown by major airlines. Traffic Alert and Collision Avoidance (TCAS), Flight Management System, and Turbulence Weather Radar are included in the avionics options, and the Engine Indication and Crew Alerting System (EICAS) uses an integrated CRT display to reduce aircraft operation and maintenance costs.

Like the Canadair Regional Jet (see below) and the Embraer EMB-145, the Saab 2000 is designed to fly longer routes than earlier-generation regional airliners. However, the duration of flights is the same — generally from 50 to 70 minutes. These aircraft simply fly faster, thus attaining greater distances within the time span of typical regional airline flights. These aircraft are designed for flight attendant service close to that of full-service airliners, but regional airline service remains similar to the shuttle service of major airlines in the Northeast Corridor, where flights typically do not include a hot meal. Flight attendants working on these aircraft can expect the usual beverage/peanut and cold snack duties, along with their standard safety role.

Passengers and flight attendants on such sophisticated aircraft as the Saab 2000, the Embraer EMB-145, the Canadair Regional Jet or the Fokker 50 will not be able to see any qualitative differences between these airplanes and the large jets flown by major airlines. The only real difference is the absence of hot meals.

Short Brothers and Others Ireland's Short Brothers, now a subsidiary of Bombardier of Canada, has been successful with its boxy, unpressurized Shorts SD3-30 and Shorts SD3-60 turboprop aircraft, placing them with such substantial U.S. regional airlines as Command Airways (an American Eagle carrier), CCAir (a USAir Express carrier) and Simmons Airlines (American Eagle). These two aircraft, which carry 30 and 36 passengers respectively, have proven themselves to be money makers in a short-haul, high-frequency business travel market.

Canadair, Short Brothers' sister company, is new in the regional airline market. The twin-engine Canadair Regional Jet, a 52-passenger, two-pilot-crew aircraft derived from the Challenger business jet, has Mach 0.8 (about 614 m.p.h.) transonic cruise speed. The first airlines adding this small jet to their fleets: SkyWest of St. George, Utah, a Delta Connection carrier; Air Nova, an Air Canada connector; British Airways; and Ansett Worldwide Aviation Services, the Australian airline company.

Fokker, the Dutch aircraft maker, followed up its F-27 turboprop and F-28 turbofan planes with the Fokker 50 turboprop and Fokker 100 turbofan. The latter has won a place in U.S. airline fleets; the former, which was the first of the regional turboprop airliners to provide big-jet luxury qualities, has done well in Europe. The Fokker 50 carries 50 passengers; the Fokker 100, a hundred passengers. The Fokker 100, of course, has full galley service, which means that hot meals can be served.

The Short Brothers and Canadair aircraft represent the old and the new of regional airline fleets. Other new aircraft: the Dornier 328, a high-speed, 29- to 33-passenger turboprop, and the British Aerospace 30-passenger Jetstream 41 turboprop. Both aircraft are large enough to require a flight attendant, whose duties embrace beverage/peanut service, an occasional cold snack, and the usual flight attendant safety role.

Large Jet Aircraft

Airbus Industrie Airbus Industrie is a consortium involving Aerospatiale (French), Aeritalia (Italian), British Aerospace (English), Fokker (Dutch) and MBB (West German). Airbus Industrie is the European competition for Boeing, McDonnell-Douglas and Lockheed.

Airbus has been highly successful with its A-300 and A-310 widebody jets and smaller A-320 jets. The A-300 series includes the A-300-B4/C4, A-300-600, A-300-600C, and A-300-600R. Passenger capacity varies from 220 to 375. The maximum length is 174.4 feet; wing span is 147.1 feet. Speed ranges from Mach 0.82 (about 629 mph) to Mach 0.86 (about 660 mph).

Of the A-310 there are four versions: the A-310-200 Standard; the A-310-200 Option; the A-310-300; and the A-310-200C.

The standard A-310-200 seats from 210 to 280 passengers. Its wingspan is 144 feet and its length 153.1 feet. Maximum cruise is at Mach 0.84.

The A-320-200 seats 140 to 179 passengers. It has a wingspan of 111.3 feet and a maximum length of 123.3 feet. Its maximum cruise is Mach 0.82.

As with other manufacturers' aircraft, the Airbus planes give flight attendants a range of working conditions, depending on whether an aircraft is an early or late model; on whether it is wide-body or narrow-body; and on how the airline has configured a particular aircraft.

Late models of the wide-bodies have an easier-to-use galley system, but the biggest differences involve configuration. There is a vast difference between an A-310-200 seating 210 passengers and the same airplane seating 280. The latter is far more crowded; passengers have less leg room and are not as comfortable; flight attendants have no more distance to traverse when catering, but they have more passengers to service while covering that distance.

Airbus planes are potentially very pleasant duty, as are Boeing, McDonnell-Douglas and Lockheed planes; a great deal depends on the airline for which a flight attendant works, for it is the airline that decides whether configuration will be strictly utilitarian or will put passengers and flight attendants at ease.

Boeing Aircraft Since 1954, when the prototype of the 707 flew, Boeing has dominated commercial flying with its succession of 700 series aircraft: 707s, 727s, 737s, 747s, 757s, 767s. Boeing even sent men to the moon in its Saturn booster, and Boeing's lunar rover carried the astronauts around on the lunar surface. The B-727 used to be the world's favorite jet, although it now is aging. The final version of this aircraft, the 727-200 Advanced, employs a cockpit crew of three, carries 145 passengers, and has a wingspan of 108 feet and a length of 153.2 feet.

The B-737 has succeeded the 727 as the most popular of all jets with the world's airlines. The latest and biggest 737 is the 737-400, which seats 159 passengers. It is 119.6 feet in length and 94.8 feet in wing span.

The newest and biggest B-747, a widebody aircraft, is the 747-400, which typically seats from 412 to 509 passengers. It has a wing span of 211 feet and a length of 231.9 feet.

The 757-200 is the standard version of the B-757 narrowbody. It carries from 186 to 220 passengers and has a wing span of 124.8 feet, a length of 155.3 feet.

The B-767 is a widebody aircraft; the latest version is the 767-300ER (extended range), which seats 204 to 290 passengers. Wing span is 156.1 feet, length 180.3 feet. The 767 is the fastest of the Boeing jets, cruising at 640 m.p.h. (well above Mach 0.8). The other Boeing jets cruise at from 575 to 600 m.p.h. (roughly Mach 0.75 to Mach 0.78).

A flight attendant working at a U.S. national or major airline is likely to do duty in any (or several) of these Boeing jets. As noted near the beginning of this chapter, the later models have a much easier catering system than the early ones have, but the biggest differences for flight attendants have to do with configuration, which varies according to the way an airline is using an airplane. For example, in its last order for B737-300 aircraft, Delta specified only 120 seats in each plane, making space for more leg room, bigger galleys and bigger closets.

The Concorde The British-French Concorde/SST (Supersonic Transport) is an aircraft with which most U.S. flight attendants will have little contact since this swift plane has won only a very limited acceptance at U.S. airports. The complaint against the Concorde is excessive noise.

With its normal cruising speed of 1,450 m.p.h. (about Mach 1.89) and its 1,894-mile range, the Concorde is used mainly for deluxe-service transoceanic flight. It has a length of 202.3 feet and a wing span of 84 feet. Seating is two-across in the slender cabin; the Concorde carries from 128 to 144 passengers.

Lockheed L-1011 and Electra The days are gone when Lockheed-California had any new commercial aircraft in the developmental pipeline, but the company maintains a presence in world airline fleets with its L-1011 TriStar widebody, three-pilot-cockpit, Rolls-Royce-powered jetliner, seating from six to nine abreast. The L-1011 has gone through several models, from the inaugural L-1011-1 through the L-1011-100, -200, -250 and -500 (the latter a long-distance version). The L-1011 has gained in maximum still-air range from 3,390 miles in the -1 version to 6,150 miles in the -500 version. The three-engine, quiet jet carries from 230 to 400 passengers, depending on model and configuration; best cruise speed is Mach 0.83 (or around 475 m.p.h.). All models except the L-1011-500 have a wing span of 155.3 feet and a length of 177.7 feet; the -500 has a wing span of 164.3 feet and a length of 164.2 feet.

Whether a flight attendant enjoys his or her work on an L-1011 depends largely on two factors. One is the airline for which the flight attendant works. Delta Air Lines, for example, has reconfigured L-1011s used on transpacific flights for a very high-quality passenger ride and correspondingly enjoyable flight attendant duties. When an airline does not go to such expense, flight attendants can find themselves having to deal with a cumbersome early galley system using an elevator, the stationing of a flight attendant in the lower lobe, and very bulky, clumsy carts.

A second factor is whether the particular L-1011 in fact uses a lower-lobe galley or whether it has a cabin-level galley. There is a world of difference between the difficulty of catering and otherwise serving an all-economy, lower-lobe-galley, 330-passenger L-1011-1; and the generally pleasurable experience of working on a full-service, cabin-level-galley, 284-passenger L-1011-250.

Lockheed's only other aircraft that a flight attendant may occasionally encounter is the old L-188 Electra turboprop, but that aircraft is rarely seen today in any use other than cargo.

McDonnell-Douglas McDonnell-Douglas, like Boeing, has a bevy of models in service. The popular DC-9 family of narrow-body jets was followed by the more modern MD-80 series; the DC-10 widebody was succeeded by the MD-11. There are six varieties of DC-8 flying, five models of DC-9 and four models of DC-10. In the 80 series, there are the MD-81, MD-82, MD-83, MD-87 and MD-88. The MD-11 comes in the basic model and the extended-range one (MD-11ER).

The DC-8 is an older-generation narrow-body jet powered by four engines at a maximum speed of about 600 m.p.h. (cruise ranges from 544 m.p.h. to 586 m.p.h., depending on the model). The wing span of the DC-8 grew from 142.3 feet in the first models to 148.4 feet in the last ones. Length grew from 150.5 feet to 187.4 feet. The final version could not only carry 259 passengers, but could handle 66,665 pounds of freight as well.

The DC-9 narrow-body, which eliminated the flight engineer required in the DC-8, was for a while the world's most popular commercial jet aircraft. Passenger capacity ranges from 85 to 135, depending on the model. Wing span of the first model was 89.4 feet; thereafter, it was 93.3 feet. Length went from 104.4 feet to 133.5 feet. The two-engine DC-9 has a best cruise speed varying from 0.76 to 0.80 Mach number (averaging about 549 m.p.h.).

The MD-81 through MD-88 have a passenger capacity of 155, with the exception of MD-87, which carries only 130 passengers. Wing span of the entire series is 107.8 feet; length is 147.9 feet except on the MD-87, which is

130.4 feet long. This follow-on series to the DC-9 cruises at 0.76 to 0.80 Mach number.

The two widebodies of McDonnell-Douglas are the DC-10 and MD-11 series. The MD-11 dispensed with the DC-10 flight engineer and achieved other efficiencies, including much greater range than the DC-10 series has. Passenger capacity of the MD-11 goes from 321 to 405, but the extended-range model carries only 277 passengers. The MD-11 is 200.8 feet long with a wing span of 169.3 feet; the MD-11ER is 182.3 feet long with a wing span of 169.5 feet. It has a range of over 8,500 nautical miles as opposed to over 8,000 for the MD-11.

CHAPTER 14
Probation, Domicile, Reserve Status

There are only a few general statements that can be made about the probationary period.

The length of probation varies. At United Airlines, it is six months; at American Airlines, eight months. Six months is fairly typical, but at some regional/commuter carriers, the time period can be less.

During probation, you may be required to pass additional exams, and you probably will be observed and evaluated while performing on the aircraft in flight. All 121 cariers are required by the FAA to provide "recurrent training" every year for flight attendants. This includes written and oral exams, updates, manual checks, and practical exams on evacuation procedures on the mock-ups.

How tough is probation? No tougher than the job itself. "Basically, if you have your head on straight, show up for work on time," one flight attendant said, "you won't have a problem."

At her company, she continued, "we had scheduled times for going in to talk with the supervisor at the base. They check your appearance, your weight, and discuss any problems you may have had."

A flight attendant at this major airline has a minimum of three check rides during probation, although the number can possibly be more, depending on whether or not a supervisor decides to take a particular flight because it happens to have three or four probationary flight attendants aboard. In that case, the supervisor would check all of the flight attendants on probation, even if one had already been checked three times.

"They have a list of items they're looking for, and they can check your in-flight manual," she said. "I think it's great. There are a lot of girls who maybe would not know they are doing things they should not be doing. We have no other way of checking. The check rides don't bother me — I'm competent and I know what to expect."

The number of weight checks during probation varies by carrier, but count on this: Your weight will be checked, and weight checks will continue throughout your career as a flight attendant.

The flight attendant quoted above noted that the job itself is physically demanding — the carts are bulky, and keeping the luggage and luggage racks in order poses a hard job for slightly built flight attendants. High-altitude flying and constant time zone changes affect your physical condition, and extremes of weather take their toll. "A lot of people feel that this is a glamorous job, and in some ways I guess it is," she said. "But I work out just about every day, not because I'm a health nut or a body builder, but I do it basically because I don't know that I could keep up with this job — having to work odd hours, long hours in any kind of weather — without being fit. Physically, this is a hard job. . . [But] I love this job. I have enough time off to do a lot of the other things that I want to do. When you get off the plane, that's the end of it. I don't take it home with me. There's even time to start your own business on the side, and a lot of flight attendants do that. . . .

"And a really wonderful part of this job is the travel privileges. I just went to Vancouver, Canada, and it will cost me about $20."

Domicile: Not in Your Control

As your initial training nears its end, where you will be based (along with the transition period that accompanies such a move) comes into sharper focus. Several factors will give you advance clues about where you most likely will be based.

For one thing, there is the bidding process itself. If more than one domicile is offered, class members will be asked to list their preferences. Bids are awarded based on seniority within the class. Seniority within a class in which all flight attendants began at the same time may be assigned by age or by such an arbitrary figure as Social Security number. A second clue is the size of the class, and a third is the number of vacancies at each domicile. Bid awards are made after the company determines how many flight attendants each domicile needs. No personal considerations sway the placement of flight attendants at each domicile; seniority alone, within the context of company need, determines who is assigned where.

Be prepared to relocate to any of your airline's domiciles. And since the time between graduation and the day you must report to your domicile is unpredictable (it can vary from one to several days), you would be well advised to have all of your personal affairs in order prior to entering training.

Many airlines provide relocation assistance, generally in the form of a salary advance, a list of available housing near the airport or a list of other airline employees desiring roommates, and on-line transportation from training to domicile.

Each airline requires its new-hires to remain in their initial domicile assignments for a specified time before they can bid on a new domicile. At any given airline, however, the domiciles available for bid will be influenced by whether a specific domicile is a senior one or a junior one. Senior domiciles are the more attractive ones, and since the flight attendants working out of such domiciles are the more senior flight attendants, openings are relatively infrequent.

Newly hired flight attendants usually are placed on reserve status. This status means that you will not have a specific advance assignment but will be "on call," filling in when and where you are needed. During your assigned duty periods, you will have to be available for any trip on short notice. Duty periods can run from eight to 24-hour shifts and from three days to a full month (a month on, a month off). Since reserves must be available on short notice, many airlines require them to live within a specified distance of the airport.

Time on reserve status can vary from one to several years, depending on the airline and the domicile. Under such circumstances, you obviously have to remain flexible. Some flight attendants "beat the rap" on domicile arrangements by using their discount air travel privileges to commute to their home towns during their off-duty periods. Commuting can be difficult, however, because time off for reserves usually is not more than nine to 11 days per month. Flying back and forth between cities can eat up most of the free time. It also means you must maintain two homes, one in your domicile city and one in your city of choice. And in reality, you will lack the seniority needed to make sure you have seats on the most convenient flights for commuting to your chosen city. You probably should not count on commuting during your first year.

A Citizen of the World

One of the most striking benefits of an airline career is the ability to travel widely. For the outsider, however, the extent of pass privileges, travel information and bargains available to airline employees is not obvious.

The privileges are essentially these: free air travel in some cases (with your own airline), deeply discounted air fares in others, and discounts on lodging, meals, and some shopping prices. The flight attendant with a major carrier who made a vacation trip from Dallas to Vancouver, Canada, for about $20 total cost to her was not an exceptional case.

A good example of pass privileges at a major airline is provided by United Airlines, where, in 1989, a brand-new flight attendant, her spouse, and her dependent children were immediately eligible for personal travel at 75 percent off. After six months, the flight attendant was eligible for an annual pass on United for simply a small service charge. Unlimited passes were available after one year of service, and the airline had an additional travel provision for parents of employees.

Information available to airline employees is extensive, to say the least. As a flight attendant, even with a regional airline, you will have access to far more information on travel bargains than does the average American; and much of the information will involve bargains that are available only to airline employees.

Your primary source of information at your airline will be the company's pass bureau. This office will be working hard to relay information on cruises and vacations to all airline employees. But you will have other sources of information, including:

- *Interline Representatives, Ltd.* Interline is considered "the airlines' personal travel agent." If you need a referral on a hotel, a booking at a vacation cottage, a rental car confirmed, or a cruise or safari planned, Interline will handle the problem for you. They have most of the needed travel information readily at hand at their New York offices. They have an 800 number for you to call.

- *ASU Travel Guide.* The grandaddy of interline travel guides is *ASU Travel Guide*. While it is expensive ($13 an issue), the *ASU Guide* contains over 300 pages of tours, resorts and discounted air fare opportunities. For a subscription, you can call their 800 number or write to their San Francisco, Calif., offices. The *ASU Guide* is especially good at locating out-of-the-way bargains, e.g., $935 for nine days in Russia, including accommodations, meals, sightseeing and transfers; or $49 per night at the Chateau Lake Louise near Edmonton, Alberta, Canada (1989 prices). Chateau Lake Louise is a grand hotel-resort in an idyllic setting for skiing.

- Intertrail. For European destinations, you could try Intertrail, from Trail Blazer Safaris of Miami, Fla. Intertrail specializes in tour programs, most of which include confirmed seats for air travel and several days of touring. Examples: five days via Air Canada to Madrid for as little as $317; or eight days in the English countryside for $564 (1989 prices).

- International airlines. Tour operators are not the only source of interline opportunities. Most international carriers offer reasonable space-available travel, round trip, from U.S. gateway cities. Eligibility varies for each carrier, but on many parents are allowed to travel with the employee. TWA, for example, was offering Eurofares for as low as $150 round trip from New York to Europe in 1989. For the more exotically minded and cash-rich, JAL was offering a $2,129 package that included a tour of China and Hong Kong.

- *Airfare* magazine. If you want a quick three- or four-day getaway, you might try one of *Airfare's* cruise tours. Headquartered in New York City, *Airfare* is a magazine that reports on discounts available to airline employees. Although not as large as *ASU Travel Guide*, *Airfare* does an excellent job of covering cruises and posting value vacations. A typical vacation is a Waikiki Beach condominium for $20 a night or a suite in Aspen for $69 a day (1989 prices).

- "Insiders Club." AirTravel Card "Insiders Club," designed for airline employees, offers its members comprehensive rental car coverage, personal accident insurance, air travel insurance, baggage coverage and medical consultation every time they fly on industry non-revenue or reduced-rate tickets. Membership in the "Insider's Club," which in 1989 cost $5 per person per year, automatically includes $100,000 of air travel insurance and worldwide medical consultation. The "Insider's Club" has a toll-free 800 number.

> A final tip to remember: Each airline has its own requirements for interline privileges as to length of employment, dependent eligibility, etc., so you should plan ahead for any travel.
>
> Within the limits of your time off (extensive), the bargains available at any given time, your personal finances, and your desire to visit different places, you are able, as a flight attendant, to be a citizen of the world. If you get a natural "high" from the ability to experience more of what the world has to offer, then you are in the right career.

The Best of Worlds

If your new job has drawbacks, some temporary, others permanent, it also has advantages that, for thousands of people, outweigh the negatives. New friends and new places, for example, are part of the allure that will cause more than 300,000 women and men to interview for the job of flight attendant this year. At large airlines like American, United and Delta, more than 30,000 people apply; around 1,000 to a maximum of 4,000 are hired (only a major airline in a big push for expansion would hire so many in one year). So you are beginning a career that many envy and would like to have. You are among the chosen few.

The best way for you to survive probation and reserve is to look upon every aspect of your new job in its most positive light.

Probation is not a time of siege (everyone wants you to succeed), but a time of implementing what you have learned in training, mending the gaps in your learning, and correcting any misconceptions you may have had. It is a time for you to be molding yourself as a career professional.

Reserve is not a penance; it is an initiation and one leg on your journey to the best that your profession has to offer.

A domicile in a city to which you are a stranger is not an exile; it is an adventure in new possibilities.

Once you are off reserve, things begin to change; you are eligible for the trip bid process, and you become a "line holder." A schedule of all trips operating from your domicile within a one-month period is issued to all flight attendants at the domicile, and all flight attendants bid on the "lines-of-flying" which they prefer. The number of bid lines is determined by the size of the base/domicile and the level of flying activity. Seniority determines who gets which trips. Trips are planned in sequence to allow days off and rest periods to give each line holder the required number of duty and off hours each month.

SEQUENCE ASSIGNMENTS

Sequence assignments are flight legs paired in series to form a daily work schedule, e.g. (three-day schedule):

Day	Equip	Route	Flt. No.	Depart	Arrive	Block to Block	Total Block	On Duty	Lay Over	
1	DC9	DTW-DCA	228	655	827	132			33	
1	DC9	DCA-BOS	228	900	1034	134			41	
1	DC9	BOS-DCA	1167	1115	1259	144			41	
1	DC9	DCA-BOS	1166	1340	1519	139			56	
1	DC9	BOS-LGA	35	1615	1729	114	743	1149	1251	Hyatt
2	DC9	LGA-MEM	631	620	825	305			45	
2	DC9	MEM-OKC	1561	910	1041	131	436	636	2138	Hilton
3	DC9	OKC-MEM	1562	819	940	121			55	
3	DC9	MEM-MOB	1562	1035	1142	107			108	
3	DC9	MOB-MEM	1544	1250	1402	112			108	
3	DC9	MEM-DTW	1041	1510	1800	150	530	956	0	

The departure and arrival times are based on the 24-hour clock. Flight 1041 departs Memphis at 3:10 p.m. and arrives in Detroit at 6:00 p.m.

Sequence assignments are available only to those flight attendants who hold "lines-of-flying."

As your seniority advances, commuting will become easier since the flights you work (routes, time of day or night) and the places you fly to are determined by your preferences and seniority. Greater seniority means that your preferences can be heeded. Your chances of having trips that fit your particular needs are enhanced; thus, commuting becomes feasible.

With advancing seniority, you also will have a greater chance of being transferred to a domicile of choice. In fact, as your seniority raises you into the upper echelons, you will reach your goal of a highly flexible, well-remunerated career punctuated by great places to see and exciting things to do.

Go for it.

CHAPTER 15

Onward and Upward

In *The U.S. Commuter Airline Industry, Policy Alternatives*, James F. Molloy, Jr. writes: "Prior to World War II, the airline industry in the United States suffered the growing pains experienced by most fledgling industries. Specifically, these were lack of recognition, early-stage technological development, and resistance from entrenched competitors. These problems were exacerbated by the fact that the aircraft of that era did not possess the capability of rendering the speed and range that have become the hallmark of this dynamic industry."

The immature state of the industry meant that the flight attendant profession, while sharing in the glamour of aviation of that period, was not truly a career path yet. All flight attendants had to be female and young (at 27, they were terminated), and they had to be registered nurses. Flight attending was something to do for adventure and for the short term.

"But by the end of World War II," Molloy continues, "the largest commercial aircraft being manufactured was the DC-4, with sixty to seventy seats, 200-plus miles per hour, and a 1,000-plus mile range. The step up to aircraft of this type by the postwar airlines appealed to the public because of the time savings over long distances. Each succeeding generation of new aircraft from that point up to the Boeing 747 tended to fly longer distances at faster speeds with increased seating capacity."

Nowadays, even the regional airlines are turning into good career stops for people who want to be flight attendants. What Molloy did not mention is that slightly faster than Mach .08 is the practical, aerodynamics-imposed upper speed limit for turbojet aircraft because of rapid losses in fuel efficiency above that point. New-generation regional aircraft — turbojet, turboprop and pusherprop — are achieving Mach .08 or slightly less, and these aircraft qualify as true airliners. They have the roomy cabins, comfort, and high-tech avionics and aircraft systems of the airplanes flown by major and national airlines. They share the marketing programs, livery and corporate image of their major airline hubbing partners. They are flying longer routes, and they are identified in the public mind with the national and international air transport systems in the United States.

The vice president of operations for a large West Coast regional airline explained the significance of substantially greater stage lengths flown by regional airlines:

"You're asking customers now to spend an hour and a half or an hour and 40 minutes in the aircraft, and you need now an effective cold snack. You need something that is what the customer expects in terms of a snack. This is one of the areas that we are striving to upgrade with the senior partners [major airlines], to give our passengers service that is comparable to what they're offering. We work many hours trying to achieve that."

The executive noted that the focus on rendering major-airline style service also involves training. "Our company is getting involved in role-playing so the agents and flight attendants can have a chance to watch their own reactions and body language in tense situations. And we're trying to teach them to understand the needs of each customer. The other sector of our business, the discretionary side of it [people traveling for pleasure instead of for business purposes], they don't always know their way around an airport, and they need more assistance. The people who can give you the most revenue [i.e., the business travelers] aren't the ones who need the most help. It's the occasional traveler who needs the most assistance during an interruption."

As airlines like this large West Coast regional grow and become identified more thoroughly with major carriers, they intensify their service training, they add more flight attendants, they pay higher salaries, they create better benefits packages for their employees — in short, as employers, they become more like the major airlines.

What the interpenetration of major and regional airlines means for you is that your career opportunities are broader than ever before. Naturally, your first choice of a job will probably be with a major or large national carrier, but if the first position that is offered to you is one with a big regional airline, you have very good reasons to accept the job. The regional airline could become a true career-choice carrier for you (an advantage of the regional carrier over the major one is that it can grant quicker promotions; you will have a better chance of moving into management, if that is your desire). If you cannot see yourself in a career at the regional airline, you win anyway, because the experience you get flying with it will help you attain your ultimate goal. Today, that goal can include annual earnings of around $50,000 a year for senior flight attendants.

To ensure that you attain your goal and hold onto it once you reach it, you need to take loving care of two items: your attitude and your health.

Attitude speaks for itself; you cannot continue to advance unless you project a positive, winning attitude.

Health requires a few words.

Two aspects of your job militate against neglect of your health: airline weight standards and the airline working environment.

Simply to maintain the correct weight as you get older, you will need to stay fit and watch your diet. To remain healthy and fit enough to perform your job properly, you must do more: You will need to inform yourself with respect to the right foods and beverages to eat and drink, and you probably will need a steady program of exercise (although not muscle-building exercise, which might add too much weight). Your diet should not only be balanced, it ought to be a low-cholesterol diet. It should not be overloaded with calcium because, while calcium is needed, too much of it tends to lead to kidney stones and other ailments. In short, what you should be seeking is a carefully balanced diet that does not go off in any extreme direction.

Your exercise program should be a running or fast-walking regimen or some other aerobic routine.

The classic prescription of a sound mind in a sound body will give you the stamina, wit and social sense necessary to advance in your chosen profession and avoid backsliding before you reach the top.

It also will enable you to enjoy what you are striving to achieve. What good are travel benefits if you feel too ill and tired to take advantage of them? What good is a lot of time off if you have to spend it recuperating for your next round of duty?

Take care of your health, your attitude and your job; take pride in your company and your profession; take the trouble to grow as a way of accepting and meeting the constant change of airline work; and make the effort to appreciate fully your job and your career. Do all of these things, and you will have a wonderful life in flight attending.

APPENDIX A

FAA Regulations Affecting Flight Attendants

(known in the industry as FARs)

Appendix A: FAA Regulations

Following are most of the FAA regulations that directly affect flight attendants. Part 91 consists of general operating and flight rules. Part 121 references the certification and operations of air carriers. Some of the rules are extracted only in part.

* 91.8 PROHIBITION AGAINST INTERFERENCE WITH CREW MEMBERS.
    (a) No person may assault, threaten, intimidate, or interfere with a crew member in the performance of the crew member's duties aboard an aircraft being operated.

* 91.11 ALCOHOL OR DRUGS
    (a) No person may act or attempt to act as a crew member of a civil aircraft:
        (1) Within 8 hours after the consumption of any alcoholic beverage;
        (2) While under the influence of alcohol;
        (3) While using any drug that affects the person's faculties in any way contrary to safety; or
        (4) While having .04 percent by weight or more alcohol in the blood.

* 91.12 CARRIAGE OF NARCOTIC DRUGS, MARIJUANA AND DEPRESSANT OR STIMULANT DRUGS OR SUBSTANCES
    (a) Except as provided in paragraph (b) of this section, no person may operate a civil aircraft within the United States with knowledge that narcotic drugs, marijuana, [or] depressant or stimulant drugs or substances as defined in Federal or State statutes are carried in the aircraft.
    (b) Paragraph (a) of this section does not apply to any carriage of narcotic drugs, marijuana, and depressant or stimulant drugs or substances authorized by or under an [sic] Federal or State statute or by any Federal or State agency.

* 91.19 PORTABLE ELECTRONIC DEVICES
    (a) Except as provided in paragraph (b) of this section, no person may operate, nor may any operator or pilot in command of an aircraft allow the operation of, any portable electronic device on any of the following U.S. registered civil aircraft:
        (1) Aircraft operated by an air carrier or commercial operator; or
        (2) Any other aircraft while it is operated under IFR [instrument flight rules].
    (b) Paragraph (a) of this section does not apply to:
        (1) Portable voice recorders;
        (2) Hearing aids;
        (3) Heart pacemakers;
        (4) Electric shavers; or

(5) Any other portable electronic device that the operator of the aircraft has determined will not cause interference with the navigation or communication system of the aircraft on which it is to be used.

(c) In the case of an aircraft operated by an air carrier or commercial operator, the determination required by paragraph (b)(5) of this section shall be made by the air carrier or commercial operator of the aircraft on which the particular device is to be used. In the case of other aircraft, the determination may be made by the pilot in command or other operator of the aircraft.

Authors' note: The three Part 121 rules that immediately follow this note are important for flight attendants because of general impact on the job of flight attending. The FAA-required manual must be carried onto all flights and kept close at hand, as noted in 121.137.

---

* 121.81 INSPECTION AUTHORITY
    (a) Each certificate holder shall allow the Administrator, at any time or place, to make any inspections or tests to determine its compliance with the Federal Aviation Act of 1958, the Federal Aviation Regulations, its [the certificate holder's] operating certificate and operations specifications, or its eligibility to continue to hold its certificate.

* 121.133 PREPARATION
    (a) Each domestic and flag air carrier shall prepare and keep current a manual for the use and guidance of flight and ground operations personnel in conducting its operations.
    (b) Each supplemental air carrier and commercial operator shall prepare and keep current a manual for the use and guidance of flight, ground operations, and management personnel in conducting its operations.

* 121.137 DISTRIBUTION AND AVAILABILITY
    (a) Each certificate holder shall furnish copies of the manual required by 121.133 (and the changes and additions thereto) or appropriate parts of the manual to:
        (1) Its appropriate ground operations and maintenance personnel;
        (2) Crew members; and
        (3) Representatives of the Administrator assigned to it.
    (b) Each person to whom a manual or appropriate parts of it are furnished under paragraph (a) of this section shall keep it up-to-date with the changes and additions furnished to that person and shall have the manual or appropriate parts of it accessible when performing assigned duties.

Appendix A: FAA Regulations

* 121.285 CARRIAGE OF CARGO IN PASSENGER COMPARTMENTS

. . . .

(c) Cargo may be carried aft of a bulkhead or divider in any passenger compartment provided the cargo is restrained to the [appropriate] load factors . . . and is located as follows:

    (1) It is properly secured by a safety belt or other tiedown [sic] having enough strength to eliminate the possibility of shifting under all normally anticipated flight and ground conditions.

    (2) It is packaged or covered in a manner to avoid possible injury to passengers and passenger compartment occupants.

    (3) It does not impose any load on seats or the floor structure that exceeds the load limitation for those components.

    (4) Its location does not restrict access to or use of any required emergency or regular exit, or of the aisle in the passenger compartment.

    (5) Its location does not obscure any passenger's view of the "seat belt" sign, "no smoking" sign, or required exit sign, unless an auxiliary sign or other approved means for proper notification of the passenger is provided.

* 121.311 SEATS, SAFETY BELTS, AND SHOULDER HARNESSES

(a) No person may operate an airplane unless there are available during the takeoff, en route flight, and landing:

    (1) An approved seat or berth for each person on board the airplane who has reached his second birthday; and

    (2) An approved safety belt for separate use by each person on board the airplane who has reached his second birthday, except that two persons occupying a berth may share one approved safety belt and two persons occupying a multiple lounge or divan seat may share an approved safety belt during en route flight only.

(b) During the takeoff and landing of an airplane, each person on board shall occupy an approved seat or berth with a separate safety belt properly secured about him. However, a person who has not reached his second birthday may be held by an adult who is occupying a seat or berth. A safety belt provided for the occupant of a seat may not be used during takeoff and landing by more than one person who has reached his second birthday.

. . . .

(d) Except as provided in subparagraphs (1) and (2) of this paragraph, no certificate holder may take off or land an airplane unless each passenger seat back is in the upright position. Each passenger shall

comply with instructions given by a crew member in compliance with this paragraph.
> (1) This paragraph does not apply to seat backs placed in other than the upright position in compliance with 121.310(f)(3).
> (2) This paragraph does not apply to seats on which cargo or persons who are unable to sit erect for a medical reason are carried in accordance with procedures in the certificate holder's manual if the seat back does not obstruct any passenger's access to the aisle or to any emergency exit.

. . . .

(f) Each flight attendant must have a seat for takeoff and landing in the passenger compartment that meets [all FAA] requirements . . . effective March 6, 1980, except that:
> (1) Combined safety belt and shoulder harnesses that were approved and installed before March 6, 1980, may continue to be used; and
> (2) Safety belt and shoulder harness restraint systems may be designed to the inertia load factors established under the certification basis of the airplane.

. . . .

(g) Each occupant of a seat equipped with a combined safety belt and shoulder harness must have the combined safety belt and shoulder harness properly secured about that occupant during takeoff and landing and be able to properly perform assigned duties.

(h) At each unoccupied seat, the safety belt and shoulder harness, if installed, must be secured so as not to interfere with crew members in the performance of their duties or with the rapid egress of occupants in an emergency.

* 121.313 MISCELLANEOUS EQUIPMENT

No person may conduct any operation unless the following equipment is installed in the airplane:

. . . .

> (g) A key for each door that separates a passenger compartment from another compartment that has emergency exit provisions. The key must be readily available for each crew member.

* 121.317 PASSENGER INFORMATION

(a) No person may operate an airplane unless it is equipped with passenger information signs that meet [all] the requirements of . . . this chapter. The signs must be constructed so that the crew members can turn them on and off. They must be turned on for each takeoff and each landing and when otherwise considered to be necessary by the pilot in command.

(b) After August 31, 1981, no person may operate a passenger-carrying airplane under this part unless there is affixed to each forward bulkhead and each passenger seat back a sign or placard that reads "Fasten Seat Belt While Seated." These signs or placards need not meet the requirements of paragraph (a) of this section.

(c) No passenger or crew member may smoke while the NO SMOKING sign is lighted and each passenger shall fasten that passenger's seat belt and keep it fastened while the FASTEN SEAT BELT sign is lighted.

* 121.333 SUPPLEMENTAL OXYGEN FOR EMERGENCY DESCENT AND FOR FIRST AID; TURBINE ENGINE POWERED AIRPLANES WITH PRESSURIZED CABINS.

. . . .

(f) Passenger briefing. Before flight is conducted . . . a crew member shall instruct the passengers on the necessity of using oxygen in the event of cabin depressurization and shall point out to them the location and demonstrate the use of the oxygen-dispensing equipment.

* 121.391 FLIGHT ATTENDANTS

(a) Each certificate holder shall provide at least the following flight attendants on each passenger-carrying airplane used:

(1) For airplanes having a seating capacity of more than nine but less than 51 passengers — one flight attendant.

(2) For airplanes having a seating capacity of more than 50 but less than 101 passengers — two flight attendants.

(3) For airplanes having a seating capacity of more than 100 passengers — two flight attendants plus one additional flight attendant for each unit (or part of a unit) of 50 passenger seats above a seating capacity of 100 passengers.

(b) If, in conducting the emergency evacuation demonstration required under 121.291(a) or (b), the certificate holder used more flight attendants than is required under paragraph (a) of this section for the maximum seating capacity of the airplane used in the demonstration, he may not thereafter take off that airplane[:]

(1) In its maximum seating capacity configuration with fewer flight attendants than the number used during the emergency evacuation demonstration; or

(2) In any reduced seating capacity configuration with fewer flight attendants than the number required by paragraph (a) of this section for that seating capacity plus the number of flight attendants used during the emergency evacuation demonstration that were in excess of those required under paragraph (a) of this section.

(c) The number of flight attendants approved under paragraphs (a) and (b) of this section are set forth in the certificate holder's operations specifications.

(d) During takeoff and landing, flight attendants required by this section shall be located as near as practicable to required floor level exits and shall be uniformly distributed throughout the airplane in order to provide the most effective egress of passengers in event of an emergency evacuation. During taxi, flight attendants required by this section must remain at their duty stations with safety belts and shoulder harnesses fastened except to perform duties related to the safety of the airplane and its occupants.

(e) At stops where passengers remain on board the aircraft and proceed on that aircraft to another destination, each certificate holder shall provide and maintain on board the aircraft during that stop at least one-half (rounded to the next lower figure in the case of a fraction) of the flight attendants as provided in paragraph (a) of this section or the same number of personnel qualified in the emergency evacuation procedures for that aircraft as required in 121.417 provided those personnel are identified to the passengers, but never fewer than one such person. These persons shall be uniformly distributed throughout the airplane to provide the most effective egress of passengers in the event of an emergency evacuation. Should there be only one flight attendant on board the aircraft, that person will be located in accordance with the airline's FAA-approved operating procedures. During such stops when the flight attendant complement is fewer than required by 121.39(a), the certificate holder must ensure that the aircraft engines are shut and at least one floor-level exit on that aircraft remains open during the stop and that such exit provides for the deplaning of the passengers.

* 121.421 FLIGHT ATTENDANTS: INITIAL AND TRANSITION GROUND TRAINING.
  (a) Initial and transition ground training for flight attendants must include instruction in at least the following:
     (1) General subjects:
        (i) The authority of the pilot in command; and
        (ii) Passenger handling, including the procedures to be followed in the case of deranged persons or other persons whose conduct might jeopardize safety.
     (2) For each airplane type:
        (i) A general description of the airplane emphasizing physical characteristics that may have a bearing on ditching,

evacuation, and inflight emergency procedures and on other related duties.

(ii) The use of both the public address system and the means of communicating with other flight crew members, including emergency means in the case of attempted hijacking or other unusual situations; and

(iii) Proper use of electrical galley equipment and the controls for cabin heat and ventilation.

(b) Initial and transition ground training for flight attendants must include a competence check to determine ability to perform assigned duties and responsibilities.

(c) Initial ground training for flight attendants must consist of at least the following programmed hours of instruction in the subjects specified in paragraph (a) of this section and in 121.415(a) unless reduced under 121.405:

(1) Group I airplanes:

(i) Reciprocating powered, 8 hours; and

(ii) Turbo propeller powered, 8 hours.

(2) Group II airplanes, 16 hours.

* 121.427 RECURRENT TRAINING

(a) Recurrent training must ensure that each crew member or dispatcher is adequately trained and currently proficient with respect to the type of airplane (including differences training, if applicable) and crew member position involved.

(b) Recurrent ground training for crew members and dispatchers must include at least the following:

(1) A quiz or other review to determine the state of the crew member's or dispatcher's knowledge with respect to the airplane and position involved.

(2) Instruction as necessary in the subjects required for initial ground by 121.415(a), as appropriate, including emergency training (not required for aircraft dispatchers).

(3) For flight attendants and dispatchers, a competence check as required by 121.421(b) and 121.422(b), respectively.

(c) Recurrent ground training for flight attendants:

(1) Group I reciprocating powered airplanes, 4 hours;

(2) Group I turbo propeller powered airplanes, 5 hours; and

(3) Group II airplanes, 12 hours.

* 121.533 RESPONSIBILITY FOR OPERATIONAL CONTROL: DOMESTIC AIR CARRIERS

. . . .

(d) Each pilot in command of an aircraft is, during flight time, in command of the aircraft and crew and is responsible for the safety of the passengers, crew members, cargo, and airplane.

(e) Each pilot in command has full control and authority in the operation of the aircraft, without limitation, over other crew members and their duties during flight time, whether or not he holds valid certificates authorizing him to perform the duties of those crew members.

* 121.542 FLIGHT CREW MEMBER DUTIES

(a) No certificate holder shall require, nor may any flight crew member perform, any duties during a critical phase of flight except those duties required for the safe operation of the aircraft. Duties such as company required calls made for such non-safety related purposes as ordering galley supplies and confirming passenger connections, announcements made to passengers promoting the air carrier or pointing out sights of interest, and filling out company payroll and related records are not required for the safe operation of the aircraft.

(b) No flight crew member may engage in, nor may any pilot in command permit, any activity during a critical phase of flight which could distract any flight crew member from the performance of his or her duties or which could interfere in any way with the proper conduct of those duties. Activities such as eating meals, engaging in nonessential conversations within the cockpit and nonessential communications between the cabin and cockpit crews, and reading publications not related to the proper conduct of the flight are not required for the safe operation of the aircraft.

(c) For purposes of this section, critical phases of flight includes [sic] all ground operations involving taxi, takeoff and landing, and all other flight operations conducted below 10,000 feet, except cruise flight.

* 121.547 ADMISSION TO FLIGHT DECK

(a) No person may admit any person to the flight deck of an aircraft unless the person being admitted is:

(1) A crew member;

(2) An FAA air carrier inspector, or an authorized representative of the National Transportation Safety Board, who is performing official duties;

(3) An employee of the United States, a certificate holder, or an aeronautical enterprise who has the permission of the pilot in command and whose duties are such that admission to the flight

deck is necessary or advantageous for safe operations; or

(4) Any person who has the permission of the pilot in command and is specifically authorized by the certificate holder management and by the Administrator.

Paragraph (a)(2) of this section does not limit the emergency authority of the pilot in command to exclude any person from the flight deck in the interests of safety.

(b) For the purposes of paragraph (a)(3) of this section, employees of the United States who deal responsibly with matters relating to safety and employees of the certificate holder whose efficiency would be increased by familiarity with flight conditions, may be admitted by the certificate holder. However, the certificate holder may not admit employees of traffic, sales, or other departments that are not directly related to flight operations, unless they are eligible under paragraph (a)(4) of this section.

(c) No person may admit any person to the flight deck unless there is a seat available for his use in the passenger compartment, except:

(1) An FAA air carrier inspector or an authorized representative of the Administrator or National Transportation Safety Board who is checking or observing flight operations;

(2) An air traffic controller who is authorized by the Administrator to observe ATC precedures;

(3) A certificated airman employed by the certificate holder whose duties require airman certificate;

(4) A certificated airman employed by another certificate holder whose duties with that carrier require an airman certificate and who is authorized by the certificate holder operating the aircraft to make specific trips over a route;

(5) An employee of the certificate holder operating the aircraft whose duty is directly related to the conduct or planning of flight operations or the inflight monitoring of aircraft equipment or operating procedures, if his presence on the flight deck is necessary to perform his duties and he has been authorized in writing by a responsible supervisor, listed in the Operations Manual as having that authority; and

(6) A technical representative of the manufacturer of the aircraft or its components whose duties are directly related to the inflight monitoring of aircraft equipment or operating procedures, if his presence on the flight deck is necessary to perform his duties, and he has been authorized in writing by the Administrator and by a responsible supervisor of the operations department of the certificate holder, listed in the Operations Manual as having that authority.

* 121.549 FLYING EQUIPMENT
    (a) The pilot in command shall ensure that appropriate aeronautical charts containing adequate information concerning navigation aids and instrument approach procedures are aboard the aircraft for each flight.
    (b) Each crew member shall, on each flight, have readily available for his use a flashlight that is in good working order.

* 121.571 BRIEFING PASSENGERS BEFORE TAKEOFF (Renumbered and revised 121-2, June 7, 1965)
    (a) Each certificate holder operating a passenger-carrying airplane shall ensure that all passengers are orally briefed by the appropriate crew member as follows:
        (1) Before each takeoff, on each of the following:
            (i) Smoking.
            (ii) The location of emergency exits.
            (iii) The use of safety belts, including instructions on how to fasten and unfasten the safety belt.
            (iv) The location and use of any required emergency flotation means.
        (2) After each takeoff, immediately before or immediately after turning the seat belt sign off, an announcement shall be made that passengers should keep their seat belts fastened while seated, even when the seat belt sign is off.
        (3) Except as provided in paragraph (a)(4) of this section, before each takeoff a flight attendant assigned to the flight shall conduct an individual briefing of each person who may need the assistance of another person to move expeditiously to an exit in the event of an emergency. In the briefing the flight attendant shall
            (i) Brief the person and his attendant, if any, on the routes to each appropriate exit and on the most appropriate time to begin moving to an exit in the event of an emergency; and
            (ii) Inquire of the person and his attendant, if any, as to the most appropriate manner of assisting the person so as to prevent pain and further injury.
        (4) The requirements of paragraph (a)(3) of this section do not apply to a person who has been given a briefing before a previous leg of a flight in the same aircraft when the flight attendants on duty have been advised as to the most appropriate manner of assisting the person so as to prevent pain and further injury.

(b) Each certificate holder shall carry on each passenger-carrying airplane, in convenient locations for use of each passenger, printed cards supplementing the oral briefing and containing:
    (1) Diagrams of, and methods of operating, the emergency exits; and
    (2) Other instructions necessary for use of emergency equipment. Each card required by this paragraph must contain information that is pertinent only to the type and model airplane used for that flight.
(c) The certificate holder shall describe in its manual the procedures to be followed in the briefing required by paragraph (a) of this section.

* 121.573 BRIEFING PASSENGERS: EXTENDED OVERWATER OPERATIONS
(a) In addition to the oral briefing required by 121.571(a), each certificate holder operating an airplane in extended overwater operations shall ensure that all passengers are orally briefed by the appropriate crew member on the location and operation of the life preservers, life rafts, and other flotation means, including a demonstration of the method of donning and inflating a life preserver.
(b) The certificate holder shall describe in its manual the procedure to be followed in the briefing required by paragraph (a) of this section.
(c) If the airplane proceeds directly over water after takeoff, the briefing required by paragraph (a) of this section must be done before takeoff.
(d) If the airplane does not proceed directly over water after takeoff, no part of the briefing required by paragraph (a) of this section has to be given before takeoff, but the entire briefing must be given before reaching the overwater part of the flight.

* 121.575 ALCOHOLIC BEVERAGES
(a) No person may drink any alcoholic beverage aboard an aircraft unless the certificate holder operating the aircraft has served that beverage to him.
(b) No certificate holder may serve any alcoholic beverage to any person aboard any of its aircraft who
    (1) Appears to be intoxicated;
    (2) Is escorting a person or being escorted in accordance with 108.21 [an FAR paragraph regulating how ill, injured or otherwise incapacitated or disabled individuals are to be handled]; or
    (3) Has a deadly or dangerous weapon accessible to him while aboard the aircraft. . . .
(c) No certificate holder may allow any person to board any of its aircraft if that person appears to be intoxicated.

206 Flight Attendant

(d) Each certificate holder shall, within five days after the incident, report to the Administrator the refusal of any person to comply with paragraph (a) of this section, or of any disturbance caused by a person who appears to be intoxicated aboard any of its aircraft.

* 121.576 RETENTION OF ITEMS OF MASS IN PASSENGER AND CREW COMPARTMENT

The certificate holder must provide and use means to prevent each item of galley equipment and each serving cart, when not in use, and each item of baggage, which is carried in a passenger or crew compartment, from becoming a hazard by shifting; the precautions mandated here must be carried out in a way that will maintain weight distribution under the appropriate load factors corresponding to the emergency landing conditions under which the airplane was type certified.

* 121.577 FOOD AND BEVERAGE SERVICE EQUIPMENT DURING TAKEOFF AND LANDING

(a) No certificate holder may take off or land an airplane when any food, beverage, or tableware furnished by the certificate holder is located at any passenger seat.

(b) No certificate holder may take off or land an airplane unless each passenger's food and beverage tray and each serving cart is secured in its stowed position.

(c) Each passenger shall comply with instructions given by a crew member in compliance with this section.

* 121.587 CLOSING AND LOCKING OF FLIGHT CREW COMPARTMENT DOOR

(a) Except as provided in paragraph (b) of this section, the pilot in command of a large airplane carrying passengers shall ensure that the door separating the flight crew compartment from the passenger compartment is closed and locked during flight.

(b) The provisions of paragraph (a) of this section do not apply

(1) During takeoff and landing if the crew compartment door is the means of access to a required passenger emergency exit or floor level exit; or

(2) At any time that it is necessary to provide access to the flight crew or passenger compartment . . . [for] a crewmember in the performance of his duties or for a person authorized admission to the flight crew compartment under 121.547.

* 121.589 CARRY-ON BAGGAGE

(a) No certificate holder may allow the boarding of carry-on baggage on an airplane unless each passenger's baggage has been scanned to control the size and amount carried on board in accordance with an approved carry-on baggage program in its operations specifications. In addition, no passenger may board an airplane if his/her carry-on baggage exceeds the baggage allowance prescribed in the carry-on baggage program in the certificate holder's operations specifications.

(b) No certificate holder may allow all passenger entry doors of an airplane to be closed in preparation for taxi or pushback unless at least one required crew member has verified that each article of baggage is stowed in accordance with this section and 121.285(c) of this part.

(c) No certificate holder may allow an airplane to take off or land unless each article of baggage is stowed:

(1) In a suitable closet or baggage or cargo stowage compartment placarded for its maximum weight and providing proper restraint for all baggage or cargo stowed within, and in a manner that does not hinder the possible use of any emergency equipment; or

(2) As provided in 121.285(c) of this part; or

(3) Under a passenger seat.

(d) Baggage, other than articles of loose clothing, may not be placed in an overhead rack unless that rack is equipped with approved restraining devices or doors.

(e) Each passenger must comply with instructions given by crew members regarding compliance with paragraphs (a), (b), (c), (d), and (g) of this section.

(f) Each passenger seat under which baggage is allowed to be stowed shall be fitted with a means to prevent articles of baggage stowed under it from sliding forward. In addition, each aisle seat shall be fitted with a means to prevent articles of baggage stowed under it from sliding sideward into the aisle under crash impacts severe enough to induce the ultimate inertia forces specified in the emergency landing condition regulations under which the airplane was type certificated.

(g) In addition to the methods of stowage in paragraph (c) of this section, flexible travel canes carried by blind individuals may be stowed:

(1) Under any series of connected passenger seats in the same row, if the cane does not protrude into an aisle and if the cane is flat on the floor; or

(2) Between a non-emergency exit window seat and the fuselage, if the cane is flat on the floor; or

(3) Beneath any two non-emergency exit window seats, if the cane is flat on the floor; or

(4) In accordance with any other method approved by the Administrator.

APPENDIX B
Flight Attendant Directory of Employers

Appendix B: Flight Attendant Directory of Employers   211

MAJOR AIRLINES:
Annual Revenue - $1 Billion +

SUMMARY

Total number of flight attendants: .... over 78,000
Total number of companies: 11
Total number of aircraft: 3,191

DIRECTORY FORMAT

Company name. Date flight ops established. Number of aircraft. Fleet. Number of flight attendants. Domiciles. Minimum requirements. Remarks. N/A = Not Available. Nepotism prohibited = Does not hire relatives. Stock exchange-stock code.

AMERICA WEST AIRLINES   1983
Fleet: 73: 2 B-747s, 4 DHC-8s, 7 B-757s, 60 B-737s. **Number of flight attendants:** 2,264. **Domicile:** Phoenix, AZ. **Minimum requirements:** Age: 23. High school. Vision: 20/40 correctable. Male/female: Ht. 60"-72", wt. in proportion. **Stock code:** OTC-AWAIRL.

AMERICAN AIRLINES   1932
Fleet: 481: 2 B-747s, 2 B-757s, 6 BAe-146s, 15 B-737s, 15 B-767ERs, 25 A-300s, 30 B-767-200s, 59 DC-10s, 163 MD-80s, 164 B-727s. **Number of flight attendants:** 11,000+. **Domiciles:** Los Angeles, San Diego, San Francisco, CA; Boston; Chicago; Dallas/Ft. Worth; Miami; Nashville, TN; New York; Raleigh-Durham, NC; San Juan, PR; Washington, DC. **Minimum requirements:** Age: 20. High school. Vision: 20/50 correctable. Male: Ht. 61 $\frac{1}{2}$"-72", wt. 130-180. Female: Ht. 61 $\frac{1}{2}$"-72", wt. 118-157. **Stock code:** NYSE-AMR.

CONTINENTAL AIRLINES   1934
Fleet: 346: 8 B-747s, 12 A-300s, 15 DC-10s, 41 DC-9s, 65 MD-80s, 99 B-737s, 106 B-727s. **Number of flight attendants:** 6,600. **Domiciles:** Cleveland, Denver, Honolulu, Houston, Los Angeles, Newark. **Minimum requirements:** Age: 20. High school. Vision: 20/20 corrected. Male/female: Ht. 62" min., wt. in proportion. **Stock code:** NYSE-TEX.

DELTA AIR LINES   1929
Fleet: 410: 30 B-767s, 36 DC-9s, 40 L-1011s, 48 MD-88s, 54 B-757s, 72 B-737s, 130 B-727s. **Number of flight attendants:** 12,000. **Domiciles:** Atlanta, Boston, Chicago, Cincinnati, Dallas, Houston, Los Angeles, Miami, New Orleans, New York, Portland, Salt Lake City, Seattle. **Minimum requirements:** Age: 20. High school. Vision: 20/20 corrected. Male/female: Ht. 72" max., wt. in proportion. **Stock code:** NYSE-DAL.

EASTERN AIRLINES   1928

Fleet: 231: 2 DC-10s, 15 L-1011s, 20 A-300s, 25 B-757s, 84 DC-9s, 85 B-727s. **Number of flight attendants:** 4,000. **Domiciles:** Atlanta, Miami, New York, Washington, DC. **Minimum requirements:** Age: 18. High school. Vision: 20/40 correctable. Male: Ht. 61"-74", Wt. 140-207. Female: Ht. 61"-74", wt. 113-165. Passport. **Stock code:** NYSE-TEX.

NORTHWEST AIRLINES   1926

Fleet: 332: 2 A-320s, 3 B-747-400s, 7 MD-80s, 8 B-747Fs, 20 DC-10s, 32 B-747s, 33 B-757s, 80 B-727s, 147 DC-9s. **Number of flight attendants:** 7,000. **Domiciles:** Boston, Chicago, Detroit, Memphis, Minneapolis, New York, Seattle. **Minimum requirements:** Age: 21. High school. Vision: 20/20 corrected. Male/female: Ht. 62" min., wt. in proportion. Passport.

PAN AMERICAN WORLD AIRWAYS   1927

Fleet: 154: 4 B-737s, 12 A-300s, 19 A-310s, 35 B-747s, 84 B-727s. **Number of flight attendants:** 4,974. **Domiciles:** London, Los Angeles, Miami, New York, Washington, DC. **Minimum requirements:** Age: 20. High school. Vision: 20/40 correctable. Male/female: Ht. 62" min., wt. in proportion. **Stock code:** NYSE-PN.

SOUTHWEST AIRLINES   1971

Fleet: 90: 90 B-737s. **Number of flight attendants:** 1,501. **Domiciles:** Dallas, Houston, Phoenix. **Minimum requirements:** Age: 20. High school. Vision: 20/20 corrected. Male/female: Ht. 62" min., wt. in proportion. **Stock code:** NYSE-LUV.

TRANS WORLD AIRLINES   1932

Fleet: 216: 12 B-767s, 18 B-747s, 33 MD-80s, 35 L-1011s, 46 DC-9s, 72 B-727s. **Number of flight attendants:** 6,000+. **Domiciles:** Los Angeles, New York, St. Louis. **Minimum requirements:** Age: 18. High school. Vision: 20/50 correctable. Male: Ht. 62"-72", wt. 127-190. Female: Ht. 62"-72", wt. 113-154. Passport.

UNITED AIRLINES   1926

Fleet: 428: 4 B-757s, 19 B-767s, 27 DC-8s, 33 B-747s, 55 DC-10s, 143 B-727s, 147 B-737s. **Number of flight attendants:** 14,000. **Domiciles:** Chicago, Cleveland, Denver, Honolulu, Los Angeles, Newark, New York, San Francisco, Seattle, Washington, DC. **Minimum requirements:** Age: 19. High school. Vision: 20/30 correctable. Male: Ht. 62"-72", max. wt. 184. Female: Ht. 62"-72", max. wt. 159. **Stock code:** NYSE-UAL.

USAir   1937

Fleet: 430: 2 F-100s, 6 B-767s, 21 BAe-146s, 31 MD-80s, 44 B-727s, 45 F-28s, 74 DC-9s, 207 B-737s. **Number of flight attendants:** 9,264. **Domiciles:** Baltimore, Boston, Charlotte, Los Angeles, Philadelphia, Pittsburgh, San Diego, San Francisco, Washington, DC. **Minimum requirements:** Age: 21. High school. Vision: 20/30 correctable. Male: Ht. 62"-75", max. wt. 220. Female: Ht. 62"-72", max. wt. 169. Wt. in proportion to ht. **Stock code:** NYSE-USAIR.

NATIONAL AIRLINES:
Annual Revenue - $100 Million to $1 Billion

SUMMARY

Total number of flight attendants: 4,705
Total number of companies: 10
Total number of aircraft: 367

DIRECTORY FORMAT

Company name. Date flight ops established. Number of aircraft. Fleet. Number of flight attendants. Domiciles. Minimum requirements. N/A = Not Available. Stock exchange-stock code.

AIR WISCONSIN (United Express) 1965
Fleet: 29: 4 SD3-60s, 10 BAe-146s, 15 F-27s. **Number of flight attendants:** 150. **Domiciles:** Appleton, WI; Fort Wayne, IN; Moline, IL; Richmond, VA. **Minimum requirements:** Age: 20. High school. Vision: 20/40 correctable. Male/female: Ht. 61"-72", wt. in proportion. **Stock code:** OTC-AIRWSC.

ALASKA AIRLINES 1932
Fleet: 50: 6 B-737s, 19 MD-80/83s, 25 B-727s. **Number of flight attendants:** 1,100. **Domiciles:** Long Beach, CA; Seattle. **Minimum requirements:** Age: 21. High school. Vision: 20/20 corrected. Male: Ht. min. 62", wt. 143 - 182. Female: Ht. min. 62", wt. 115 - 171. **Stock code:** NYSE-ALK.

ALOHA AIRLINES 1946
Fleet: 14: 14 B-737s. **Number of flight attendants:** 180. **Domicile:** Honolulu. **Minimum requirements:** Age: 18. High school. Vision: 20/50 correctable. Male/female: Ht. 62" min., wt. in proportion. Passport.

AMERICAN TRANS AIR 1973
Fleet: 18: 8 B-727s, 10 L-1011s. **Number of flight attendants:** 400. **Domiciles:** Boston, Chicago, Dallas, Detroit, Indianapolis, Las Vegas, New York. **Minimum requirements:** Age: 18. High school. Vision: 20/40 correctable. Male/female: Wt. in proportion to ht. Passport.

BRANIFF 1928
Fleet: 59: 1 A-320, 25 B-727s, 33 B-737s. **Number of flight attendants:** 965. **Domiciles:** Dallas/Ft. Worth, Kansas City, Ft. Lauderdale, Orlando. **Minimum requirements:** Age: 20. High school. Vision: 20/20 corrected. Male/female: Ht. 62"-76", wt. in proportion. **Stock code:** OTC-BRANIF.

HAWAIIAN AIRLINES 1929
Fleet: 27: 5 L-1011s, 6 DC-8s, 6 DHC-7s, 10 DC-9s. **Number of flight attendants:** 650. **Domiciles:** Honolulu, Los Angeles, Philadelphia, San Francisco, Seattle. **Minimum requirements:** Age: 18. High school. Vision: 20/20 corrected. Male/female: Ht. 62"-72", wt. in proportion. Passport. **Stock code:** AMEX-HAL.

HORIZON AIR 1981
Fleet: 39: 2 F-28s, 3 F-27s, 8 DHC-8s, 26 SA-227s. **Number of flight attendants:** 70. **Domiciles:** Boise, ID; Portland, OR. **Minimum requirements:** High school. Vision: 20/20 corrected. Wt. in proportion to ht.

MARK AIR 1947
Fleet: 6: 1 DHC-7, 5 B-737s. **Number of flight attendants:** 50. **Domicile:** Anchorage, AK. **Minimum requirements:** Age: 21. High school. Vision: 20/20 corrected. Male/female: Ht. 62" min., wt. in proportion.

MIDWAY AIRLINES 1979
Fleet: 63: 4 MD-87s, 10 B-737s, 20 DO-228s, 29 DC-9s. **Number of flight attendants:** 1,000. **Domiciles:** Chicago (Midway Airport), Philadelphia. **Minimum requirements:** Age: 21. High school. Passport. Vision: 20/20 corrected. Male/female : Ht. 62" min., wt. in proportion. **Stock code:** NYSE-MDWY.

WESTAIR/UNITED EXPRESS 1978
Fleet: 62: 5 SD3-60s, 6 BAe-146s, 6 BA-3101s, 15 EMB-120s, 30 EMB-110s. **Number of flight attendants:** 140. **Domiciles:** Fresno, Long Beach, Los Angeles, San Francisco. **Minimum requirements:** Age: 21. High school. Vision: 20/40 correctable. Male/female: Ht. max. 68", wt. in proportion. **Stock code:** OTC-WSTAIR.

TURBOJET AIRLINES:
Annual Revenue - Less Than $100 Million

SUMMARY

Total number of flight attendants: 1,508
Total number of companies: 17
Total number of aircraft: 124

DIRECTORY FORMAT

Company name. Date flight ops established. Number of aircraft. Fleet. Number of flight attendants. Domiciles. Minimum requirements. N/A = Not Available.

AIR AMERICA 1978
Fleet: 1 DC-9. **Number of flight attendants:** 30. **Domicile:** Detroit. **Minimum requirements:** Wt. in proportion to ht.

AIRLIFT INTERNATIONAL 1983
Fleet: N/A. **Number of flight attendants:** 7. **Domiciles:** Ft. Lauderdale/Miami. **Minimum requirements:** High school. Wt. in proportion to ht. Passport.

ASPEN AIRWAYS 1953
Fleet: 14: 4 BAe-146s, 10 CV-580s. **Number of flight attendants:** 64. **Domicile:** Denver. **Minimum requirements:** Age: 21. High school. Vision: 20/20 corrected. Wt. in proportion to ht.

ATLANTIC AIRLINES 1979
Fleet: 7: 2 DC-9-10s, 5 IAJ-1121s. **Number of flight attendants: 8. Domiciles:** Chicago, Dallas-Ft. Worth, Los Angeles, Orlando. **Minimum requirements:** Age: 18. High school. Vision: 20/20 corrected. Male: Ht. 60"-70", wt. 100-170. Female: Ht. 60"-68", wt. 90-130. Passport.

EMERALD AIR 1978
Fleet: 5 DC-9s. **Number of flight attendants:** 40. **Domicile:** Atlantic City. **Minimum requirements:** Age: 19. High school. Vision: 20/20 corrected. Male: Ht. 65"-75", wt. 130-205. Female: Ht. 60"-75", wt. 90-170. Passport.

EXPRESS ONE 1980
Fleet: 28 B-727s. **Number of flight attendants:** 69. **Domiciles:** Dallas, Philadelphia. **Minimum requirements:** Age: 21. Two years college. Male/female: Ht. min. 5'2", wt. in proportion. Passport.

INDEPENDENT AIR 1970
Fleet: 2 B-707s. **Number of flight attendants:** 40. **Domicile:** Atlanta. **Minimum requirements:** Age: 21. Two years college. Male/female: Ht. min. 62", wt. in proportion.

KEY AIRLINES 1979
Fleet: 9: 1 DC-10, 8 B-727-100s. **Number of flight attendants:** 162. **Domiciles:** Las Vegas, Los Angeles, New York. **Minimum requirements:** Age: 21. High school. Male/female: Ht. min. 62", wt. in proportion. Vision: 20/50 correctable. Passport.

MIDWEST EXPRESS AIRLINES 1984
Fleet: 11 DC-9s. **Number of flight attendants:** 102. **Domicile:** Milwaukee. **Minimum requirements:** Age: 20. High school. Vision: 20/50 correctable. Male/female: Ht. min. 62", wt. in proportion.

NORTH AMERICAN 1989
Fleet: 1 B-757. **Number of flight attendants:** 30. **Domicile:** New York (JFK). **Minimum requirements:** Age: 20. High school. Vision: 20/50 correctable. Male: Ht. 63"-74", wt. 150-207. Female: Ht. 63"-74", wt. 121-165. Passport.

PRESIDENTIAL AIRWAYS   **1985**
Fleet: 3 DHC-8s. **Number of flight attendants:** 36. **Domicile:** Washington-Dulles. **Minimum requirements:** Age: 21. High school. Vision: 20/30 correctable. Male/female: Ht. 62"-74", wt. in proportion. Passport.

RICH INTERNATIONAL AIRWAYS   **1970**
Fleet: 3 DC-8s. **Number of flight attendants:** 85. **Domicile:** Miami. **Minimum requirements:** N/A.

SUN COUNTRY AIRLINES   **1983**
Fleet: 4: 1 DC-10, 3 B-727s. **Number of flight attendants:** 68. **Domicile:** Minneapolis. **Minimum requirements:** High school. Vision: 20/20 corrected. Male/female: Wt. in proportion to ht. Passport.

TOWER AIR   **1983**
Fleet: 4 B-747s. **Number of flight attendants:** 252. **Domiciles:** Miami, New York, Tel Aviv. **Minimum requirements:** Age: 18. High school. Vision: 20/20 corrected. Male: Ht. 62"-74", wt. 120-185. Female: Ht. 62"-74", wt. 100-154. Passport.

TRANS CONTINENTAL   **1975**
Fleet: 2 DC-8s. **Number of flight attendants:** 35. **Domicile:** New York (JFK). **Minimum requirements:** Age: 18. High school. Vision: 20/30 correctable. Wt. in proportion to ht. Passport.

TRANSOCEAN AIRWAYS (formerly Gulf Air)   **1979**
Fleet: 9: 5 B-727s, 4 DC-8s. **Number of flight attendants:** 200. **Domiciles:** Boston; Chicago; New York (JFK); Philadelphia. **Minimum requirements:** Age: 20. High school. Vision: 20/20 corrected. Male/female: Ht. 62"-74", wt. in proportion. Passport.

TRUMP SHUTTLE   **1989**
Fleet: 21 B-727s. **Number of flight attendants:** 280. **Domiciles:** New York (LGA), Washington, DC, Boston. **Minimum requirements:** Age: 18. High school. Vision: 20/40 correctable.

REGIONAL AIRLINES: Propeller Driven Aircraft

SUMMARY

Total number of flight attendants: 1,360
Total number of companies: 21
Total number of aircraft: 542

DIRECTORY FORMAT

Company name. Date flight ops established. Number of aircraft. Fleet. Number of flight attendants. Domiciles. Minimum requirements. N/A = Not Available.

AIR MIDWEST 1967
Fleet: 14: 7 EMB-120s, 7 SF-340s. **Number of flight attendants:** 48. **Domicile:** St. Louis. **Minimum requirements:** Age: 19. High school. Vision: 20/20 corrected. Male: Ht. 67" max., wt. 155 max. Female: Ht. 67" max., wt. 135 max. **Stock code:** OTC - AMWI.

ATLANTIC SOUTHEAST AIRLINES 1979
Fleet: 54: 5 DHC-7s, 11 EMB-110s, 38 EMB-120s. **Number of flight attendants:** 146. **Domiciles:** Atlanta, Macon, GA; Dallas, TX. **Minimum requirements:** Age: 21. High school. Vision: 20/20 corrected. Male/female: Ht. minimum 62", wt. in proportion. **Stock code:** OTC - ASAI.

BAR HARBOR AIRLINES/CONTINENTAL EXPRESS 1968
Fleet: 33: 6 SF-340s, 6 BE-99s, 10 ATR-42s, 11 BE-1900s. **Number of flight attendants:** 67. **Domiciles:** Bangor, ME; Newark. **Minimum requirements:** Age: 19. High school. Vision: 20/20 corrected. Male/female: Ht. 72" max., wt. in proportion.

BUSINESS EXPRESS 1984
Fleet: 31: 4 SD3-60s, 5 F-27s, 6 SF-340s, 16 BE-1900s. **Number of flight attendants:** 70. **Domiciles:** Boston; Bridgeport, Hartford, New London, CT; Manchester, NH; Islip, NY. **Minimum requirements:** Age: 19. High school. Vision: 20/20 corrected. Male/female: 60" min., wt. in proportion.

CHAUTAUQUA AIRLINES 1974
Fleet: 12: 2 SF-340s, 3 BE-99s, 7 SA-227s. **Number of flight attendants:** 6. **Domiciles:** Canton/Akron, OH; Jamestown, NY. **Minimum requirements:** Age: 19. High school. Vision: correctable to 20/40. Male/female: Ht. 60"-68", wt. in proportion.

COMAIR   1977
Fleet: 51: 12 EMB-110s, 17 SF-340s, 22 SA-227s. **Number of flight attendants:** 58. **Domiciles:** Cincinnati; Orlando. **Minimum requirements:** Age: 21. High school. Vision: correctable to 20/30. Male/female: Ht. 62"-67", wt. in proportion. **Stock code:** OTC - COMR.

COMMAND AIRWAYS   1969
Fleet: 21: 5 ATR-42s, 9 SD3-60s, 7 SD3-30s. **Number of flight attendants:** 85. **Domiciles:** Albany, Poughkeepsie, NY; Boston; Washington, D.C. **Minimum requirements:** Age: 21. High school. Vision: correctable to 20/50. Wt. in proportion to ht.

CROWN AIRWAYS   1969
Fleet: 3 SD3-30s. **Number of flight attendants:** 22. **Domiciles:** DuBois, PA; Parkersburg, Youngstown, WV. **Minimum requirements:** Age: 21. High school. Male/female: Ht. 62"-74", wt. in proportion.

EXPRESS AIRLINES I   1985
Fleet: 38: 12 SF-340s, 26 BA-3101s. **Number of flight attendants:** 59. **Domiciles:** Memphis, Minneapolis. **Minimum requirements:** Age: 19. High school. Vision: 20/20 corrected. Male/female: Ht. 62"-69", wt. in proportion.

HENSON AIRLINES/USAIR EXPRESS   1967
Fleet: 33: 6 DHC-7s, 27 DHC-8s. **Number of flight attendants:** 155. **Domiciles:** Florence, SC; Norfolk, VA; Jacksonville, FL; Salisbury, MD; New Bern, NC. **Minimum requirements:** Age: 21. High school. Vision: 20/20 corrected. Male/female: Ht. 63"-70", wt. in proportion.

LAREDO AIR   1988
Fleet: 4: 2 CV-440s, 2 CV-580s. **Number of flight attendants:** 6. **Domicile:** Atlantic City. **Minimum requirements:** Age: 20. High school. Vision: 20/20 corrected. Male/female: Ht. 73" max., wt. in proportion.

MESABA AIRLINES   1943
Fleet: 15 F-27s. **Number of flight attendants:** 54. **Domiciles:** Detroit, Minneapolis. **Minimum requirements:** Age 18. High school. Vision: 20/20 corrected. Male: Ht. 62"-72", wt. 130-185. Female: Ht. 62"-72", wt. 105-165. Able to lift 75 lbs. **Stock code:** OTC - AIRTRAN.

METRO AIRLINES NORTHEAST   1968
Fleet: 10 SF-340s. **Number of flight attendants:** 39. **Domicile:** S. Burlington, VT. **Minimum requirements:** Age: 18. High school. Male/female: 72" max., wt. in proportion.

METROFLIGHT   1969
Fleet: 20 SF-340s. **Number of flight attendants:** 60. **Domicile:** Dallas. **Minimum requirements:** Age: 20. High school. Vision: 20/20 corrected. Male: Ht. 61"-68", wt. 160 max. Female: Ht. 61"-68", wt. max. 141. **Stock code:** OTC-METAIRL.

Appendix B: Flight Attendant Directory of Employers

NASHVILLE EAGLE   1979
Fleet: 49: 14 SA-227s, 15 SA-226s, 20 BA-3100s. **Number of flight attendants:** 10. **Domiciles:** Nashville; Raleigh-Durham; Miami. **Minimum requirements:** Age: 20. Wt. in proportion to ht.

PAN AM EXPRESS   1967
Fleet: 22: 10 DHC-7s, 12 ATR-42s. **Number of flight attendants:** 126. **Domiciles:** Los Angeles; Philadelphia; Providence, RI. **Minimum requirements:** Age: 21. High school. Vision: 20/20 corrected. Male/female: Ht. min. 61", wt. in proportion. Passport.

PENNSYLVANIA AIRLINES   1965
Fleet: 7: 3 SD3-30s, 4 SD3-60s. **Number of flight attendants:** 34. **Domiciles:** Middletown/Harrisburg, State College, Williamsport, PA. **Minimum requirements:** Age: 21. High school. Vision: correctable to 20/30. Male: Ht. 61"-74", wt. 133-208 Female: Ht. 61"-74", wt. 113-172.

ROCKY MOUNTAIN AIRWAYS   1965
Fleet: 26: 6 DHC-7s, 10 ATR-42s, 10 BE-1900s. **Number of flight attendants:** 58. **Domicile:** Denver. **Minimum requirements:** Age: 21. High school. Vision: correctable to 20/40. Male/female: Ht. 62"-72", wt. in proportion.

SIMMONS AIRLINES   1978
Fleet: 47: 14 ATR-42s, 33 SD3-60s. **Number of flight attendants:** 165. **Domicile:** Chicago. **Minimum requirements:** Age: 21. High school. Vision: 20/20 corrected. Male/female: Ht. 60"-72", wt. in proportion.

SKYWEST   1972
Fleet: 39: 9 EMB-120s, 30 SA-226/227s. **Number of flight attendants:** 32. **Domiciles:** Palm Springs, CA; Salt Lake City. **Minimum requirements:** Age: 19. High school. Vision: 20/20 corrected. Male: Ht. 62"-68". Female: Ht. 60"-67". Wt. in proportion to ht. **Stock code:** OTC-SKW.

USAIR EXPRESS/ALLEGHENY COMMUTER AIRLINES INC.   1957
Fleet: 13: 3 F-27s, 5 SD3-60s, 5 SD3-30s. **Number of flight attendants:** 60. **Domiciles:** Atlantic City, NJ; Allentown, Harrisburg, Lancaster, Reading, Wilkes Barre/Scranton, PA. **Minimum requirements:** Age: 21. High school. Male/female: 62"-74", wt. in proportion.

A GLOSSARY OF USEFUL TERMS

Glossary

Aborted takeoff/aborted landing: The interruption of an aircraft's normal takeoff or landing procedure.

Air sickness: Motion sickness suffered by air travelers. Symptoms are nausea and light-headedness.

Air Traffic Control: FAA radio communication facilities charged with safe guidance of aircraft through the nation's air space and on the ground at airports.

AFA: Association of Flight Attendants.

APA: Allied Pilots Association. Union representing American Airlines pilots.

APFA: Association of Professional Flight Attendants.

Base: See "domicile."

Belly: Lower lobe of an aircraft, used for cargo, landing gear and galleys (sometimes).

Bidding: The process of establishing a work schedule, on a seniority basis and for a definite period of time.

Buffet: Area of an aircraft for storing catering supplies.

Bulkhead: A partition dividing the passenger cabin; sometimes removed, as in all-coach service.

Capacity: Maximum number of passengers and crew that can be carried on an aircraft.

Captain: The flight officer in command.

Carrier unit: Removable buffet compartments for storing food, beverages, catering supplies.

Configuration: The arrangement of seats, bulkheads, baggage bins, restrooms, etc., in the interior of an aircraft.

Control Tower: A structure reaching above the airport complex from which FAA Air Traffic Control personnel operate. See Air Traffic Control.

Crew complement: Number of crew members assigned to work any given flight.

Deadhead: Transport of an off-duty crew member on an airplane (or in ground transportation) on return from a flight assignment.

Decompression: Sudden lowering of air pressure in the cabin, leaving air pressure the same outside and inside the aircraft.

Ditching: Emergency landing on water.

Domicile: The town at which a flight attendant or pilot is based for scheduling and flight purposes. This town may or may not be the community in which the flight attendant or pilot lives.

Duty time: Time for which a flight attendant is paid; begins when a flight attendant reports to work, ends when debriefing is finished.

ETA: Estimated time of arrival.

Federal Air Regulations (FARs): Rules enforced by the Federal Aviation Administration to guard against safety hazards.

Feed traffic: Passengers brought to a major airline by a regional/commuter airline. Major carriers maintain hubs at large airports. Many small airlines have contracts with the major carriers to supply these hubs with "feed" from small towns in exchange for various benefits, often including joint marketing, use of the major's CRS (computer reservations system), some ground handling, the display of certain insignia of the major airline, ticketing at some stations, and a pro rata share of through-fare revenues.

First officer: The copilot.

Flight station: Flight officer or flight attendant jump-seat area.

Flow plan: An organized system for in-flight services.

Galley: That part of an airplane where food is stored. Food and beverage service is distributed from the galley.

Greenwich Mean Time (GMT): Reference local time at the Prime Meridian in Greenwich, England. This serves as the basis for time calculation around the world.

Hub airport: An airport at which one or more major airlines have established service hubs, i.e., clearing sites for traffic. An airline's routes branch out in "spokes" from the "hub" to form a service "wheel." This kind of operation, a product largely of airline deregulation, has proven to be the most efficient method of moving both people and cargo by air.

Hypoxia: Lack of oxygen in the blood; prevalent after decompression.

IFFA: Independent Federation of Flight Attendants.

Inflight Services: Department responsible for the care administered to passengers aboard an aircraft.

International dateline: An imaginary line drawn north and south through the Pacific Ocean, largely along the 180th meridian. It is the line at which, by international agreement, each calendar day begins at midnight. When it is Sunday just west of the line, it is Saturday just east of it.

IUFA: Independent Union of Flight Attendants.

Jet escape door: Emergency exit used only in an evacuation.

Jump seat: Located by emergency exits, this is a seat in which a flight attendant sits during takeoffs and landings.

Layover: Crew rest break between flight assignments.

Lead flight attendant: Crew member in charge of in-flight services and staff.

Lower-lobe galley: Kitchen facilities in the belly of an aircraft, a story below the main passenger cabin. Found on wide-body aircraft.

Major airline: A commercial airline with more than $1 billion in annual revenue (U.S. Department of Transportation's definition).

Narrow-body: Term to describe an aircraft with a single aisle dividing the passenger seats.

National airline: A commercial airline with revenue from $100 million to $1 billion (U.S. Department of Transportation's definition).

Official Airline Guide: Reference book listing the schedules of all flights on commercial airlines in the U.S. and abroad (except the U.S.S.R.).

Passenger service unit: A panel within reach of the passenger seat that houses an air vent, a call button, a reading light and supplemental oxygen supplies.

Piston-engine aircraft: Also called "reciprocating engine" aircraft. These are propeller-driven aircraft that are powered by piston engines.

Pressurize: To keep nearly normal (ground-level) atmospheric pressure inside an airplane, i.e., at high altitudes or in rising or descending.

Purser: Supervisor of in-flight crew and services on international flights.

Range: Distance that can be flown by an aircraft.

Regional/commuter airline: An airline with less than $100 million in revenue (U.S. Department of Transportation definition).

RON: Remain Overnight. This is "legal" rest at hotel accommodations away from home domicile.

Second officer: The flight engineer in a three-person airplane crew.

Seniority: Pay, work assignments, promotions, benefits, etc., are pegged to seniority, based on date of hire. The more senior flight attendants not only make more money but are more likely to get the aircraft, route and scheduling assignments of their choice.

Shoulder harness: Restraining strap worn by crew members in a jump seat.

Slide: Inflatable chute used during emergency evacuations to get passengers and crew safely from the aircraft to the ground.

Teamsters, International Brotherhood of, Airline Division: Union organization representing pilots, professional flight engineers and flight attendants of several airlines.

Time zone: A 15-degree segment of Earth's surface.

Turbojet aircraft: Jet airplanes. The turbojet or turbofan engine propels the aircraft with a jet of forced air. The engine continuously generates tremendous compression and heat in its compressors; this is the energy that drives the aircraft.

Turbojet airline: A jet carrier with less than $100 million in revenue (a distinction made by some in the airline industry, including Future Aviation Professionals of America).

Turboprop aircraft: Aircraft powered by turbine engines that circulate hot, compressed air through a series of ducts, generating the force necessary to turn the propeller or propellers of the aircraft. Like the turbofan engine, the turboprop engine runs on a fuel akin to kerosene.

Twenty-Four-Hour Clock: Clock used in the military, the airline industry and for other purposes; each hour of the day has an assigned number from one to 24.

UFA: Union of Flight Attendants.

Wide-body: Term describing an aircraft with two aisles dividing the passenger seats.